Great British TV Quiz Shows

By
Tony Nicholson

FOREWORD BY
CHRIS TARRANT

GREAT NORTHERN

Great Northern Books
PO Box 1380, Bradford,
West Yorkshire, BD5 5FB

www.greatnorthernbooks.co.uk

© Tony Nicholson 2023

Design, illustration and layout by David Burrill.

ISBN: 978-1-914227-48-6

CIP Data
A catalogue for this book is available from the British Library

Contents

FOREWORD

BY CHRIS TARRANT

Everybody loves a quiz. Quizzes feed the very human trait of wanting to be right all the time. Through our lives we all accumulate huge quantities of facts, trivia and knowledge, most of it completely and utterly useless in everyday life, and much of it never ever used again, but a quiz allows us to make use of all that otherwise yawn-inducing information. Sometimes for praise from others, but often, if alone in your car, or in front of the telly, just for your own smug satisfaction.

It's almost impossible to see or hear a quiz question on

TV or radio and not try to answer it yourself. Correct answers often seem to come out of nowhere. It's extraordinary how something that you've not thought about for even a second since you left school, maybe thirty or more years ago, suddenly comes to the forefront of your brain. This happened to me a lot during the fifteen years I hosted *Who Wants to Be a Millionaire?* I very deliberately never saw the questions before the show, so mentally I'd be working them out at the same time as the contestant.

I remember one question that came up about a particularly unattractive woman, painted by Holbein. I knew instantly that the answer was Anne of Cleves, and, without giving anything away on my face, I was just mentally urging the guy opposite me to just say "Anne of Cleves, final answer", and he would have won a quarter of a million pounds. Eventually he said "Catherine Parr", and lost an eye-watering £100,000. The computer said the answer was Anne of Cleves, I knew it was Anne of Cleves, I would honestly have staked my life on it being Anne of Cleves, and, of course, I was right, it was Anne of Cleves. My point is not to tell you what a clever dick I am, but, driving home after the programme, I remember thinking what an extraordinary creation the human brain is. Where on earth did that information lie in storage all this time? I hadn't thought about Anne of Cleves since my history 'O level', and that was nearly fifty years ago.

David Briggs – the guy who came up with the idea for *Who Wants to Be a Millionaire?* and dozens of other quizzes for radio, my producer on *Millionaire*, and also for twenty years my producer at Capital Radio – always loved to create what he called 'shout-ability'. People would be crawling into London in their cars, I would be asking general knowledge questions to a contestant on the phone and people would be screaming the answer out loud at the radio, even though I obviously couldn't hear them. And, of course, with *Who Wants to Be a Millionaire?* David created the ultimate pinnacle of 'shout-ability'. All over the world audiences in their homes would shout the answers to every question, sometimes arguing heatedly amongst themselves and also hurling dreadful abuse at any contestant who could clearly be seen to be struggling with an answer.

Richard Madeley's wife, Judy Finnigan, told me once that Richard would scream obscenities, some of which she'd never even heard from his lips before, at some poor hapless contestant dithering on the screen before him, and my mum told me that my dear, polite, soft-spoken dad would get into a rage of frustration, screaming 'thicko' (and sometimes far worse!) at any contestant who was faltering.

Thousands upon thousands of people take part in pub quizzes every single week. It's a great way for a pub to fill the place during the normal midweek lull in the drinking and dining trade. I've staged large-scale pop and general knowledge quiz nights for various charities over the last twenty years or so. They're an absolute hoot, getting the most extraordinary reaction from otherwise normally well-behaved adults, and they raise a lot of money for some very good causes.

These charity quiz nights have been some of the wildest events I have ever hosted. At one large hotel venue in the Channel Islands the panic-stricken catering manager had to intervene on health and safety grounds because half of the by now well-oiled and, in many cases, distinctly overweight, members of the audience, had taken to dancing on the rather flimsy tables.

At another one of these elegant, sophisticated charity soirees, men running up to the front of the room with their answer sheets at the end of each round were rugby-tackled to the ground by a rival group of somewhat ample ladies to slow them down.

It would be fair to say that *Who Wants to Be a Millionaire?* is inarguably the most successful quiz format in global television history. To the shame and disbelief of America, who really invented the television quiz show, they missed the biggest one of all. *Millionaire* was invented here in little old Britain, and sold to over 120 countries, including America, as well as Australia, Austria, and Afghanistan (and that's just the A's!).

It's not always about the money though. In some of our most successful quiz formats it's still just about the glory of winning by knowing it all. To this day the ultimate prize for the series champion on *Mastermind* is a cut-glass bowl. Although *Millionaire* does have the most simple but brilliant format, which is why it has worked so well everywhere around the world, I'm not at all sure that we would have had the same level of success on ITV with *Who Wants to Be a Cut-Glass Bowl Owner*.

I never set out to be a quiz show host, it just sort of happened somehow. In fact, back in the days of *Tiswas*, and some of my early radio shows, we would regularly send up the whole genre of quiz and gameshows, and a particular breed of really smarmy TV show hosts, who seemed to arrive on our screens, hand-in-hand with the advent of the television quiz in this country.

When I was still at school a man called Hughie ("and I mean that most sincerely friends") Green seemed to front almost every quiz show on television. My mum always called him 'oily', my dad hated him, and I remember thinking he was probably not a very nice man. When, years later, I met him in real life, I have to say he was so much worse than I had expected.

Nevertheless, I really enjoy the job, despite some very dodgy role models. Giving Judith Keppel a million pounds for getting fifteen answers correct was one of the biggest thrills of my working life. I should add though that it wasn't always the huge sums that gave me the most satisfaction. Giving a little old lady £8,000 to pay off all her debts and, just for once, get a bit ahead of the game was equally satisfying. Giving people life-changing sums of money for knowing correct answers is a tremendous privilege. However, for the contestants, it's still almost as satisfying to go home with the much-coveted cut-glass bowl as a million pounds. Well, I did say 'almost'.

One of the most memorable quiz shows I have ever watched was on television in Kenya. After several nights of nail-biting intellectual cut and thrust, the ecstatic winner went home, to the envy of the runners-up, with his hard-won prize. It was a torch.

Tony's well-researched book is a fascinating history of the evolution of the TV quiz show. He and I have worked together on many television and radio gameshows, over rather more years than either of us cares to remember. Some of them were absolutely brilliant and some were truly awful.

INTRODUCTION

Quiz shows have been a popular staple on British television ever since the birth of ITV in 1955. The evolution of them is fascinating, but at the heart of them all is the very simple premise of a question on a particular subject being answered correctly or incorrectly. Quizzes are perennially popular. Pub quizzes have probably never been better attended than they are today, an event where the know-it-all is king (or queen). The pub bore suddenly becomes the pub hero!

I suppose one of the main attractions is competitiveness. We all like to win. In sport it is only the gifted and super-fit who can hope to hold a trophy aloft, but a quiz allows the rest of us mere mortals to have a chance at victory. Even the idlest couch potato can be a champion when it comes to a quiz.

Trivial Pursuit has been one of the most popular new board games of recent years, and, let's face it, that's basically a do-it-yourself takeaway quiz show.

It's hardly any wonder therefore that, still to this day, quizzes are some of our favourite television programmes. I have been involved behind the scenes in quite a few of them over the years, including the Rolls Royce of all quiz shows – *Who Wants to Be a Millionaire?*

The best gameshows and quiz shows are those where you can play along at home, and feel part of the event as it happens. Once again we love to show off if we know the answers. We have to let everybody know just how clever we are. It makes us feel good about ourselves. We also inexplicably find we have a burning desire to shout at the TV set, whether it's the answer to the question, or just friendly advice to the contestant – "Take the money, you clueless clot!" … "Phone a friend, you silly chump!" (You will of course realise, dear sensitive reader, that I have cleaned those up for the sake of common decency in print.)

This book is not exactly a complete history of the UK quiz show, and it's certainly not an encyclopaedia, or a dry, dusty reference book on the subject. But it is an affectionate and personal guide to the evolution of seven decades of TV quizzes in the UK, from the baby steps of *Take Your Pick* and *Double Your Money*, to present-day classics, like *The Chase* and *Eggheads*, plus other current quiz show hits. It inevitably allows me, along the way, to talk in depth about the extraordinary journey to Britain's jewel in the quiz show crown, *Who Wants to Be a Millionaire?*

You will have to forgive me for writing with my tongue straying into my cheek at times, and taking an unapologetically jaundiced look at some of the shows. It's not a subject to take too seriously after all, and this isn't an academic thesis or a dissertation for a doctorate on the subject. (Not only that, but there have been some real turkeys over the years!)

Please don't write to tell me I've missed quite a few TV quizzes. I already know! There will be quite a lot which don't get a look-in, for all sorts of reasons. For example, ITV's short-lived late night quiz *Fact Hunt* won't be getting a mention, purely because of its sniggeringly juvenile cheap-joke title.

I'm sorry though if I happen to have overlooked one of your favourites.

However, I do aim to talk about all the quiz shows which have been a significant stepping-stone in the gradual evolution of the genre, and others that have brought an ingenious new dimension to a straightforward quiz, refreshing and revitalising the genre, and helping keep it alive. I make no apologies for majoring on *Millionaire*, partly because I was there and know quite a lot about it, but mainly because it was undoubtedly the most important quiz show ever created, and had a momentous impact on the future of all other TV quizzes.

For over forty years I have been a television producer/scriptwriter and now, somewhat reluctant to retire, I find myself to be an author. I have teamed up with Chris Tarrant (and others) on a lot of quiz and gameshows over the years, including *Millionaire*. I have watched TV quiz and gameshows all my life, so I am writing as a genuine fan of the genre, as well as a protagonist and TV professional. (If you are thinking that Richard Osman would be better qualified to write this book, you are probably right, but he's ever so busy!)

NOTE – I have had to make a distinction between quiz and gameshows. Quiz shows involve straightforward questions and answers, with a reward for being correct. The TV 'gameshow' is a much broader canvas, and quite possibly another follow-up book! *Blind Date* was a gameshow, and so is *I'm a Celebrity Get Me Out of Here*. Gameshows can involve anything from guessing visual or verbal clues in shows like *Catchphrase* and *Blankety-Blank*, to tests of skill, like physical prowess and dexterity, improvised acting or making things, on shows like *Gladiators*, *The Cube*, *The Generation Game* and *Bake Off*.

Admittedly there is a grey area in between – programmes like *Bullseye*, *Tipping Point* and *Sale of the Century*, which contain a quiz/general knowledge element, often to earn the right to play the skilled part of the game. Comedy gameshow formats, like *Celebrity Squares*, also contain a general knowledge question-and-answer element. I will dip into those, if and when it suits me. It's my book, so I make the rules.

It does mean there will be a few surprises, even shocks. For example, you may be surprised to find that Sir Bruce Forsyth hardly gets a mention. Brucie was, without doubt, king of the gameshow, but he didn't really do quizzes. His forte was teasing the contestants, and getting the comedy out of ordinary people and celebrity guests on non-quiz games and physical challenges, like *Beat the Clock*, *Play Your Cards Right*, *Strictly*, and his opus magnum, *The Generation Game*.

This book is predominantly about quiz shows on British television, but, inevitably, there are some inextricable links to American TV quiz shows, so again I will refer to those from time to time. And I can't miss the chance to talk about the two biggest quiz scandals in television history – *Twenty-One* in America, the quiz series which was axed because the producers were secretly feeding a particular contestant the answers to the questions, just to keep him on the show … and, of course, Chris Tarrant's unseemly brush with 'The Coughing Major', who very nearly cheated his way to one million pounds…

TAKE YOUR PICK

It is argued by some that the first TV quiz in the UK was a strange programme on the BBC, dating right back to 1938, called *Spelling Bee*. I don't personally subscribe to that theory, because it wasn't a question-and-answer quiz, it was a glorified spelling test, and, in those very early experimental days of television, it wouldn't have been particularly glorified. In any case, hardly anybody in Britain had a television set until the 1950s, so the viewers were probably about fifteen techno nerds from the BBC itself. There were no recordings in those days, so there's nothing in the BBC archive. Consequently, I'm going to draw a discreet veil over *Spelling Bee* and its host, Freddie Grisewood, dressed as he apparently was in a schoolmaster's mortarboard and gown.

The first fully-fledged quiz/gameshow to appear on British television was *Take Your Pick*, hosted by Michael Miles, which first aired in 1955. It was the year of the launch of ITV, the UK's first ever commercial television station. In fact *Take Your Pick* was first broadcast in September that year, their first month on air, and it was an instant success, with massive viewing figures.

The show itself had several quite different elements.
To get a chance at the serious money a contestant first had to survive the *Yes-No Interlude*.

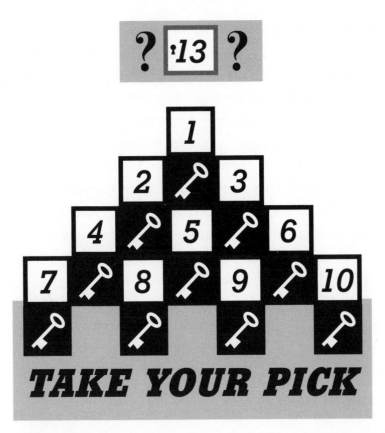

TAKE YOUR PICK

The next round featured a rising pyramid of ten numbered compartments, each containing a key. This is where the quiz element came in. A single contestant stood by the pyramid and was asked four general knowledge questions by Michael Miles. If they answered at least three correctly then they were given the chance to pick a number, and therefore a key. The keys opened boxes at the left-hand side of the studio, each containing a card detailing the mystery prize associated with that number. Even Michael Miles didn't know which prize card was in which box.

To attract advertisers ITV needed to create shows which were real people-pleasers and would pull in vast audiences. Famously the fledgling ITV did a deal with Val Parnell, the boss of the legendary Moss Empires variety theatre circuit, to make one of their first ever mega-ratings hits, *Sunday Night at the London Palladium*, hosted in its first incarnation by chirpy comedian Tommy Trinder, "You lucky people!" That show featured all the top variety stars from around the world and proved to be hugely popular. The Beatles famously headlined the show in 1963 and the hysteria outside the Palladium that night is widely regarded as marking the start of 'Beatlemania'.

In their desire for shows that would appeal to the ordinary working men, women and children of Britain, ITV decided they wanted a gameshow where members of the public could win cash and prizes. Remember there were still only two British TV channels in those days, and the BBC, up to that point, had never wanted to be associated with anything so vulgar. They were still quaking in the shadow of their first ever Director General, the somewhat puritanical Lord Reith, whose mission statement for the BBC was that it was there to "inform, educate and entertain". Because he was somewhat strait-laced and from a privileged upper-class background, his idea of entertainment was certainly not dancing girls, broad comedy and common people winning filthy money. During every episode of *The Wall* and *Mrs Brown's Boys* Lord Reith can be heard slowly revolving in his grave.

Take Your Pick had been a successful reward quiz/gameshow in sound-only on Radio Luxembourg since 1952, so it was a prime candidate to be adapted for

The host was an avuncular middle-aged chap, a New Zealander called Michael Miles. To be honest, by today's standards, he looked more like a bank manager than a gameshow host, but that was the way of television in those days. In any case he had devised the show, so it was his baby, right from its first outings on Radio Luxembourg.

It was rumoured that Michael Miles was tricky to work with, but Jane Murray, one of his non-speaking female hostesses, later revealed that he secretly suffered from epilepsy, which possibly accounted for his irascible moods.

television by ITV. In fact it was to be the first ever TV show in Britain to offer cash prizes. (Just three days later Hughie Green's *Double Your Money* became the second.)

The *Yes-No Interlude* was a cleverly addictive game where the host, Michael Miles, would ask each contestant simple quickfire questions about themselves for sixty seconds. That would have been really easy, if it wasn't for the fact that they weren't allowed to answer 'yes' or 'no', nor were they allowed to shake their head or nod. Try it sometime – it's much more difficult than you'd think.

There was a little bespectacled chap called Alec Dane, hovering ominously on the other side of the contestant with a gong. He was the umpire and would take great delight in bashing his gong if the nervous punter slipped up.

Many would be 'gonged off' within seconds...

Michael – You are Gladys from Birmingham?

Gladys – Yes

Alec – GONG!!

If she was shrewd enough to say "That's right", she could still easily go on the next question...

Michael – Nice to meet you Gladys. Are you well?

Gladys – Yes, thank you...

Alec – GONG!!

The host's famous trick, if they were doing quite well at the game, would go something like this:

Michael – What do you do for a living?

Contestant – I'm a bus driver.

Michael – A bus driver?

Contestant – Yes...

Alec – GONG!!

Even if the contestant was smart enough to answer "That's correct", then Michael would enquire, "You didn't nod your head then did you?" Invariably they would indignantly shake their head and say "No".

It's a wonder anybody ever got through to the next round. If they did survive the whole minute then Michael would reward them with the princely sum of five shillings, which is twenty-five pence in current decimalised currency. Can you imagine trying to give a TV gameshow winner twenty-five pence these days? You would end up with the shape of your cranium moulded into Alec Dane's gong. Admittedly earlier I estimated a 28 times inflation rate, since those days. Even so, 25 pence would only be the equivalent of seven quid today. I still think you would get the gong over your head!

TAKE YOUR PICK

In the main game, with the ten numbered boxes, the randomly distributed prizes were three worthless 'booby prizes', one 'treasure chest' of fifty pounds cash, one 'star prize' of a small car or a holiday, plus five decent prizes of expensive household goods or quality personal items. These could be things like a three-piece suite or a washing-machine. They may not sound like life-changing prizes now, but you have to remember that the 1950s was a period of post-war austerity and people were used to 'making do'. New furniture or futuristic, new-fangled kitchen appliances genuinely were regarded as rare luxury items for ordinary people.

One added twist was that one of the pyramid compartments contained two keys – the numbered key associated with that compartment, plus the key to 'Box 13', which contained either a really valuable prize, or another 'booby prize'. Thirteen being unlucky for some, as they say. This was another gamble. If they chose to "open the box" then Michael would open their numbered box, and Box 13, which contained a cryptic verbal clue to the mystery prize it was hiding. Now they had three choices – they could take the prize in their chosen number box, or they could risk that the clue in Box 13 was leading towards an even better prize, or they could take yet another cash incentive that Michael was offering to buy back the key to Box 13. You could see the beads of sweat, even on the tiny grainy black-and-white screens we all had in those days.

The 'booby prizes' were silly things like a used teabag, a prune, a mousetrap, or, if you were really lucky, a feather duster.

Before the numbered box was opened to reveal their mystery prize, Michael would attempt to buy the key off the contestant, offering increasing amounts of hard cash, in return for their key. This presented a huge dilemma for the player, which made for good television. (As we will see – watching contestants make difficult decisions is a major factor in any successful quiz format.) There was a three-in-ten chance their key wasn't worth a carrot, but then it might just be the key to "Tonight's star prize". Michael would start offering them maybe a fiver for their key, which was easy to refuse, but then he might offer £20, then £30. That was a lot of money to turn down in those days. Whether they took his cash offer or not, Michael couldn't wait to disclose what prize was inside their box. Imagine the gasps when they'd accepted thirty pounds, but Michael revealed that they would have won the car if they'd been brave enough to hold out. And imagine the even bigger gasps if they'd turned down anything up to £50 hard cash, only to find they were going home with a shrivelled prune as a 'booby prize', worth absolutely nothing. It was riveting television, and set the benchmark for tension and jeopardy in nearly every quiz and gameshow which followed.

The gamble did get slightly easier for later contestants, providing they had paid attention to which of that night's prizes had already been won.

Take Your Pick also sparked the use of audience participation catchphrases. Michael, when he'd made his final attractive cash bribe, would ask: "What should she do?" and the audience would shout back either "Take the money!" or "Open the box!" Bruce Forsyth was no doubt watching and learning.

Just to prove how dedicated I was to television shows, in particular *Take Your Pick*, I must tell you that, as a very young boy, I spent hours building a somewhat rough-and-ready replica of the show's key pyramid out of painted cardboard cartons, so that I could host my own version of *Take Your Pick* at home. I was a strange child!

The unseen announcer was the famous voice of Bob Danvers-Walker. Famous because, for thirty years, he was the unmistakable and reassuringly British voice of the oft-repeated and fondly mimicked Pathé Newsreel clips.

Bob used to start *Take Your Pick* by introducing "Your quiz inquisitor, Michael Miles!" For some reason that catchphrase really resonated with me and stuck in my head for years. Although I thought he was saying "Your quiz and quizitor" (whatever a quizitor is!) I assumed it was like an interrogator, so I wasn't too far from the truth. Michael would then bound on to a fanfare played on the organ by Harold Smart.

Michael Miles' own company produced the shows, adding to his income as deviser and host of the show. It was said at the time that he was earning the phenomenal sum of £20,000 a year from *Take Your Pick*, which, according to my earlier calculation about the value of sterling in 1955, would be the equivalent of well over half a million pounds nowadays.

His version of this classic quiz show ran for nearly thirteen years, and was only cancelled then because broadcasters, Associated Rediffusion, lost their ITV franchise to Thames Television.

Take Your Pick was revived in the 1990s by Des O'Connor, with his wife-to-be, Jodie Wilson, as his co-host, but somehow the re-hashed show never quite had the magic of its pioneering and ground-breaking first outing. In fairness a lot of bigger and brasher quizzes had come along by then, so maybe it couldn't hope to square up to the more contemporary formats.

The original version though was an astonishing start to the popular TV genre that was going to become so important to British viewers...

Take Your Pick created a template for quiz shows for many years to come, with glamorous female hostesses bringing on the contestants, and taking them off again when they had won ... or lost.

DOUBLE YOUR MONEY

Contestants chose a specialist subject from 42 categories on the board, then answered questions on that subject. If they answered a question correctly, they could either take the cash or try to answer the next question for double money. The first question was for a pound, and was jokey and very easy. The next question, on the same subject, for £2, was a fraction harder, but still not terribly challenging. Of course, as the money kept doubling, so did the difficulty of the questions. The cut-off point was £32 – a significant sum in those days. A £32 winner was given the opportunity to return the following week to have a crack at the elimination question for *The Treasure Trail*, where they could win up to a massive £1,000.

The second pioneering gameshow to be launched by ITV, in its first month on air, was *Double Your Money*, hosted by Hughie Green. In fact it was the first true thoroughbred general knowledge quiz show. The first ever transmission was broadcast just three days after the first outing of *Take Your Pick*. Again, it was a transfer from Radio Luxembourg, where the quiz had been a big hit since 1950. The format was based on an American radio quiz called *Take It or Leave It*, which changed its name in 1968 to *The $64 Dollar Question*, eventually evolving into the more famously opulent *$64,000 Dollar Question*.

The idea was, like most successful TV formats,

15 FILMS
16 FARMING
17 FOOTB...
18 GENE...
19 GEOG...
20 GARD...
21 GOO...
22 GRA...
23 HIST...
24 HORSE...
25 LAW, CRIMIN...
26 LITERATURE
27 LONDON
28 MOTORINO

remarkably simple. A contestant answers a general knowledge question. If they get it wrong they leave empty-handed, but if they get it right they have a dilemma. They can either take the cash that question was worth, or they can risk losing that money by having a go at answering the next question. The temptation to take that risk is great, of course, because the next question is worth double the money.

That simple premise has been at the heart of many quiz/reward shows over the years, notably *Who Wants to Be a Millionaire?*

There was a peculiar mix of question categories to choose from, including: farming, babies, boxing, housekeeping, opera and dogs. The first question was for a pound, and was usually a corny joke, dressed up as a question, with a painfully obvious answer. It was virtually impossible NOT to win a pound.

Hughie Green is often described as being Canadian, but he was actually born and brought up in south-east England. He developed his well-known brash mid-Atlantic accent during an extensive tour of Canada as a teenager, with his own concert party, followed by a spell in the Canadian Air Force, during the Second World War.

The host put in a less than subtle performance, mugging to camera at every opportunity. Hughie arguably was the first to give 'the gameshow host' an archetypal reputation

THE
£1000
TREASURE TRA

for smarm, which wasn't helped by his unconvincing catchphrase, "I mean that most sincerely friends". But he was hard to ignore, and did have a distinctive personality. He was very much a man of the people though, and audiences seemed to love him.

Hughie was very shrewd and recruited his 'glamorous' assistants from contestants who had appeared on the show, including an elderly working-class lady called Alice Earrey, and, more notably, a chirpy Cockney sixteen-year-old called Monica Rose. She was a tiny little thing, barely four-foot-nine, but what she lacked in height, she made up for with broad grins, sassy personality and cheeky charm. Audiences loved her!

What is less well known is that one of the show's first hostesses was twenty-year-old Margaret Smith. Her quiz show hostessing career was short-lived, however, as her day job started to get in the way. Her name may not mean much to you, until I tell you that she is now better known as national treasure, Dame Maggie Smith, renowned star of *Downton Abbey* and countless hit films and stage plays.

> After the first shows they had their own signature tune composed, with the lyrics:
>
> *Double Your Money and try to get rich,*
>
> *Double Your Money, without any hitch,*
>
> *Double Your Money, it's your lucky day,*
>
> *Double Your Money and take it away!*
>
> I don't think it won too many Grammys or Golden Globe awards.

To win the massive jackpot prize of £1,000 the successful contestant who reached *The Treasure Trail* was seated in a soundproof capsule. Ostensibly this was to keep them isolated from distractions, and from any audience help, but there were rumours that the soundproof box was deliberately ill-ventilated to make it hot and uncomfortable, allowing the viewer to see them sweating and squirming under pressure. The questions very often had multiple-part answers, so you really had to know your stuff to win £1,000 – the highest cash prize given on British TV for many years. It's hard to imagine what the thousand-pound multi-part question on babies would have been. Bear in mind, in those days, you certainly couldn't talk about how babies are made.

Like *Take Your Pick* Hughie's quiz show came to an end in 1968, during the big ITV franchise shake-up. However, new franchise holders Yorkshire Television came to the rescue and breathed temporary new life into the old format in 1971, by re-jigging it as *The Sky's the Limit*...

THE SKY'S THE LIMIT

As before, answering general knowledge questions correctly led to increasing cash prizes – up to £100 now, instead of £32. Again the top cash-winning contestants were given the opportunity to end up in the old soundproof booth for a chance of winning better and better holidays, answering travel and geography questions. The top jackpot prize was 21,000 travel miles, with £600 spending money.

The travel theme was maybe a bit limiting, because it wasn't as successful as its predecessor, and it led to the inclusion of a lot of cheesily naff elements. Hughie was referred to as the 'Flight Controller', the contestants were introduced as 'passengers', and the hostesses were dressed as faux air stewardesses. Well, it was the seventies...

The only other three things I remember about Hughie Green are:

- His long-running talent show *Opportunity Knocks*, with its famous 'Clapometer'.
- The fact that a shock DNA test revealed him to be Paula Yates' father.
- An extraordinary right-wing nationalistic rant that he inexplicably came out with at the end of one particular show in 1976. Check it out on YouTube, complete with triumphant fanfares and rousing choral singing.

ASTRONOMY
ATHLETICS
BALLET
BIBLE

THE SKY'S THE LIMIT

This re-vamp of *Double Your Money* starred Hughie Green once again, who also brought along his comedy sidekick Monica Rose as one of his female co-hosts. The format was basically the same, but the big difference was that it was all travel-themed.

Whether Hughie Green liked it or not he had created a monster by nurturing young Monica Rose. The public adored her, and didn't really want to see him without her. They became a highly unlikely double act, even appearing on the Royal Variety Performance together, and singing a duet on record, as well as travelling overseas to showcase Double Your Money. For a time nobody wanted Hughie without his funny little Cockney sidekick. Inevitably her overnight fame and showbusiness career was relatively short-lived, as there was little else she had to offer, and Hughie had other fish to fry. He was probably keen for people to remember him as a solo performer and presenter.

It must have been a lot to take in for a very young teenager, going from life on a rough London council estate, hopping on the bus to work, to being a TV star, picked up by a chauffeur in a Rolls Royce and flying on private planes ... and then losing all that glamour, wealth and fame again, just over ten years later. She'd had it long enough to get used to it, but she was still way too young to retire on it.

Back in the real world she suffered from depression and other severe mental health issues, although she did find religion and a loving husband away from the bright lights of TV. Tragically though she lost the battle with her demons and took her own life in 1994, aged just 45.

Showbusiness can be a very cruel and unforgiving mistress sometimes.

SPOT THE TUNE

A simple twist on the classic general knowledge question-and-answer quiz came along in 1956, again on ITV. This time it involved music, provided by the studio orchestra and resident singer Marion Ryan (mother of Sixties pop star twins, Paul & Barry Ryan).

The original host was comedian Ken Platt. He was followed by a TV newcomer, then calling himself Desmond O'Connor. Later hosts included comedy actor Alfred Marks, Canadian pop singer Jackie Rae, comedian Ted Ray and DJ Pete Murray. Marion Ryan remained a constant throughout.

The show was a massive success and ran for over six years. A similar American format, *Name That Tune*, was successfully brought back to ITV screens in 1976, hosted by genial comedian, and master of the gameshow, Tom O'Connor.

Contestants had to identify a famous piece of music by listening to just a few bars from the tune, played by the studio orchestra and sung by Marion Ryan. They were against the clock, so they could be timed out.

Just as a point of social history, I remember Marion Ryan being gossiped about and frowned upon as something of a shameful 'scarlet woman', at the time, because she was a divorced single mother, and it was revealed that she had been heavily pregnant with her twin sons when she got married. How far we have come (thank goodness!) in a relatively short space of time, in terms of tolerance and morality. These days the children are often the bridesmaids and pageboys at their proud parents' weddings.

CRISS CROSS QUIZ

By 1957 ITV was pushing the boundaries of quiz shows and adding new twists and other elements to refresh and revitalise the genre. One of the first was an idea imported from America, which had been seen over there as *Tic-Tac-Dough*. It was a question-and-answer quiz imposed upon the simple age-old paper-and-pencil game 'Noughts & Crosses' (aka 'Tic-Tac-Toe', in the States).

Each of the eight outer squares added £10 to your prize pot, and the tougher-to-answer centre square was worth £20. (As the show became more successful these sums were increased to £20 and £40.) This meant that a good reigning champion could return week after week and accumulate ever-increasing cash, with no top limit. This eventually created a moral dilemma. One multi-returning champion managed to amass a staggering £2,360, which caused a bit of a furore in the press, so a cap of £1,000 for all UK TV cash prizes was introduced, which wasn't raised until 1960.

This was the start of an ongoing battle between ITV and their regulatory body, the IBA (later renamed the ITC). ITV were constantly pushing for a relaxation on the rigidly imposed upper limits for cash prizes.

Criss Cross Quiz was hosted for all its first five years by actor Jeremy Hawk, who often played the straightman/stooge/comic feed to many of the top comedians of the day – notably Norman Wisdom, Arthur Askey and Benny Hill.

CRISS CROSS

£ 80 QUIZ

POLITICS	THEATRE	USA
✕		
FAIRY TALES	**LONDON**	**NICKNAMES**
	◯	
WOMEN	**ANIMALS**	**AVIATION**
✕	◯	✕

A studio board displayed a traditional noughts & crosses style grid of nine squares, but each square was marked with a question subject category. Each week the reigning champion took on a new challenger and tried to make a line of three crosses, opposed by the noughts of the other contestant. To win the right to put an O or an X on the board you had to correctly answer the question on the subject associated with your chosen square. An incorrect answer put your opponent's symbol in that square. If the challenger managed to create a row of three noughts, in any direction, then they became the new reigning champion.

Original host Jeremy Hawk handed the show over briefly to TV journalist Bill Grundy, but Bill was replaced after a year by Canadian-born actress, TV panellist and presenter Barbara Kelly, who kept the show alive until 1967.

There was also a 'children's hour' version called *Junior Criss Cross Quiz* which had over ten hosts across the years, including the adult show presenters Jeremy Hawk, Bill Grundy, and Barbara Kelly, plus an early starring role for children's TV legend Bob Holness.

Needless to say, the junior contestants were playing for points rather than hard cash, but of course we all know what points make (thanks Brucie!) – yes, prizes.

The same basic principle of a noughts & crosses quiz was given a showbiz twist by Bob Monkhouse in 1975, with a comedy/celebrity game called *Celebrity Squares*. (*Hollywood Squares* in the US.)

DOTTO

Another crowd-pleasing twist on the straightforward general knowledge quiz came a year later in 1958, with a show called *Dotto*. It was another neat American idea, which combined answering questions with the perennially popular concept of joining up dots to create a picture.

Two contestants were faced with the same seemingly random fifty dots which, when joined up, created a cartoon drawing of a famous face. Often the eyes and hair were already inked-in, to give them a good start. If they answered a general knowledge question correctly they won the chance to magically join up several of the dots. There were varying difficulties of questions, so, if you chose to answer a hard question, and got it right, you joined up more dots.

The two contestants were positioned at separate boards round a ninety-degree corner from one another, so that they couldn't see each other's dots and lines. It was a race therefore to guess the famous face. It paid to guess correctly as soon as possible, firstly to beat your opponent, but also because every remaining dot on your board, that hadn't yet been joined up, won you £5.

It was hugely successful and had that always popular selling-point of the 'play-at-home' factor. A bit like *Catchphrase* these days, viewers would be desperately trying to guess the drawing before the contestants in the studio. Even if they couldn't answer the general knowledge questions anybody could have a go at guessing who the slowly emerging drawing was.

The UK hosts were Robert Gladwell, followed by actor Jimmy Hanley (father of *Magpie*'s Jenny Hanley), and finally it marked an early TV appearance of Shaw Taylor, later famous for the long-running real-life crime-solving series *Police 5*, ITV's forerunner to *Crimewatch*.

Like many gameshows and quiz shows *Dotto* was an American format. On the other side of the pond though it had come to a very abrupt and rather embarrassing halt. It seems some American TV producers were less scrupulous than squeaky-clean producers over here, and didn't apparently have the same sense of traditionally British fair play. They were more keen to please their sponsors and advertisers and, in the search for the best possible television output, they were, shall we say, manipulating both the contestants and the outcomes.

Contestants were not just being carefully selected and screened, but they were being groomed, coached and fed lines and stage directions to create greater tension in the studio. In some cases they were blatantly employing actors to play the parts of contestants. *Dotto* was found guilty of this sort of match-fixing. Worse still though, one contestant, who presumably the producers believed would make 'good television' as a winner, was discovered to be carrying a notebook with the answers to all that night's questions, carefully written out for her by the *Dotto* production team. The whistle-blower was a fellow 'stand-by' contestant who found the evidence and made the shocking discovery. The producers tried to give him $1,500 to buy his silence. Unfortunately for them he didn't remain silent, and he squealed like a stuck pig.

The American television networks (CBS and NBC), who broadcast both a daytime version and an evening version of the show, were hugely embarrassed when this all came out, and they axed the show with immediate effect.

In fairness the UK version carried on, untainted by this scandal, as it was being produced fairly over here. Shaw Taylor would have grassed them up to the rozzers if they'd tried anything!

It turned out that *Dotto* wasn't the first, and certainly not the only TV quiz in America, to be using these highly dubious tactics to massage the results and get the winners they wanted. Further investigations by New York prosecutor Joseph Stone led to the producers of six quiz shows having to face a Grand Jury, which, in turn, led to American Congress amending legislation to make gameshow fixing illegal.

Before computer graphics the lines appeared by magic, courtesy of two stagehands, made invisible by being dressed from head to toe in black, joining the dots with marker pens on the other side of the two translucent screens.

TWENTY-ONE

At this point it's probably worth a quick diversion to talk about American TV quiz show *Twenty-One*, because, even though it was never a format adopted by British TV, it was the worst offender in the big 1950s US quiz show scandal.

The show had been devised by its original host Jack Barry. The idea was that the winner received $500 for every point they were ahead of their rival at the end of the game. So, if the final score was 21–13, the winner accumulated $4,000. That way a good multi-returning reigning champion could rack up a lot of money quite quickly.

At first the game was played honestly and fairly, but, when the first two contestants proved to be rather dull and pretty hopeless at answering quiz questions, one of the show's producers proclaimed the show a dismal failure. The series sponsors were furious. The solution was simple … but dishonest!

The quiz was loosely based on the card game, Pontoon, where the aim is to get a perfect score of twenty-one. Two contestants, in isolation booths, so they were unaware of each other's progress, answered quiz questions, trying to be the first to reach a score of twenty-one. The winner stayed on as reigning champion, to take on a new contender.

From that point on it was decided that *Twenty-One* should be cast like a play, choreographed, manipulated, almost scripted, to guarantee successful contestants and gripping tension. Some contestants were treated pretty much like actors and were told when to answer correctly, and also which questions to get wrong. Of course this sometimes meant giving them the answers, so they were all in on the scam. They were even told when to mop their brows and look stressed. Jack Barry always claimed that he was kept blissfully unaware of what was going on right under his nose. He was still ultimately tainted by the scandal, however.

One smug reigning champion (Herbert Stempel) became unpopular with viewers, so the sponsors wanted rid of him. A highly intelligent college professor called Charles Van Doren was brought in as a 'ringer' to unseat the champion. At first this proved difficult because Stempel's genuine knowledge kept forcing a draw, despite the help Van Doren was receiving behind closed doors. This tense rivalry proved popular for a while, but, in the end, Stempel was instructed to take a dive and was told to deliberately answer one particular question incorrectly, which he reluctantly did, against all instincts and sense of fair play. Somehow though he still managed yet another draw. The disliked but brainy champion was defeated in the next game by Van Doren. Charles later admitted though that the show's producers had not only been telling him the questions, but they were also supplying him with the correct answers.

The new reigning champ, Charles Van Doren, proved to be much more popular with the public, and viewing figures sky-rocketed. With a little help from his friends, including the answers to many more questions, he managed to return for a record-breaking fourteen weeks, accumulating a staggering total of $129,000, and becoming a star of American television and darling of the media in the process. A very disgruntled Herbert Stempel blew the whistle though and a federal investigation was instigated. At first the producers denied any wrongdoing, and Stempel was accused of jealousy and being a sore loser.

When the whole 1950s US quiz show scandal erupted though, with *Dotto* being pulled from American schedules,

Stempel's accusations against *Twenty-One* began to be taken more seriously. The whole story played out in front of a Grand Jury. Other contestants admitted to being helped to cheat by the producers, and *Twenty-One* was unceremoniously cancelled. The show's producers were disgraced, becoming persona non grata in the American TV industry, and legislation was changed to make what they'd done illegal.

In 1994 Robert Redford directed a hugely-successful Oscar-nominated film called *Quiz Show*, which was based on the true story of the *Twenty-One* quiz show scandal.

UNIVERSITY CHALLENGE

Meanwhile, here in the UK, perhaps seeing where quizzes were disastrously going awry in America, and the potential pitfalls of shows offering massive financial rewards, we were becoming less brash and commercialised with our quiz show output. ITV rather turned its back on the vulgarity of shows offering high value prizes. Their next big quiz idea was surprisingly intellectual and rather worthy.

Based on an American idea called *College Bowl*, Granada TV, rather surprisingly, launched *University Challenge* on ITV in 1962. It was hosted by the rather staid and schoolmasterly Bamber Gascoigne. The series, which was only initially slated to be a trial series of thirteen programmes, was a surprise hit with a cult following, and survived for twenty-five years on ITV, all 913 episodes being hosted by Bamber.

In 1987 ITV decided it was perhaps too intellectual for the people's channel and it was cancelled. However,

Teams from two British universities compete answering quickfire general knowledge questions.

Each team comprises four students, all hailing from the same university.

The series is a simple knockout tournament, with losing teams being eliminated and winners going forward to quarter-finals, semi-finals and one grand final to find the ultimate winning university.

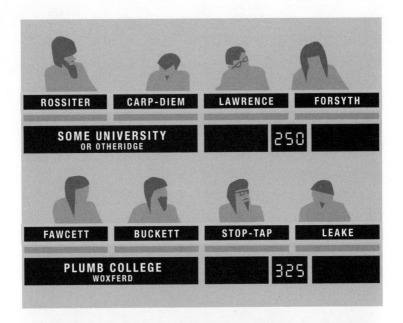

ROSSITER	CARP-DIEM	LAWRENCE	FORSYTH

| SOME UNIVERSITY OR OTHERIDGE | | 250 | |

FAWCETT	BUCKETT	STOP-TAP	LEAKE

| PLUMB COLLEGE WOXFERD | | 325 | |

> *University Challenge* was, and still is, famous for its double-decker, two-tier formation of the competing teams. In fact the effect is a TV illusion, created using split-screen technology.

University Challenge was revived in 1994. ITV regional franchise holders Granada TV were still producing the show, but now it was, rather confusingly, making the show for the BBC. It is said that Bamber Gascoigne was too busy to re-apply for his old job, so the role of quizmaster went to the redoubtable no-nonsense hardman of journalism Jeremy Paxman.

At the time of writing this book the series is still ongoing, which makes it by far the longest-running British quiz show of all time.

MPSON FRY

Several then unknown students who appeared on the show as youthful, if earnest team members went on to become famous in their own right, including – Clive James, Stephen Fry, Miriam Margolyes, former Tory cabinet minister David Mellor, revered television news journalist John Simpson and Julian Fellowes, creator and writer of *Downton Abbey*.

Although Bamber Gascoigne was very much a serious quizmaster, and not a classic gameshow host, he did, rather surprisingly, have a list of regular catchphrases: "Your starter for ten, no conferring" … "Fingers on buzzers" … and … "I'll have to hurry you!"

And not many people know that he once wrote a hit West End comedy revue called *Share My Lettuce*, which starred Kenneth Williams and Maggie Smith in the sketches.

TOP OF THE FORM

Having talked about *University Challenge*, we should perhaps briefly mention *Top of the Form*, which actually predates everything we have discussed so far. It started

Teams from two British secondary schools competed answering quickfire general knowledge questions.

Each team comprised four schoolkids, aged between 13 & 17, all hailing from the same school.

The series was a simple knockout tournament, with losing teams being eliminated and winners going forward to quarter-finals, semi-finals and a grand final to find the ultimate winning school.

as a radio quiz on the BBC's Light Programme, as far back as 1948, but didn't transfer to BBC TV until 1962, hosted by Geoffrey Wheeler, the same year as the launch of *University Challenge*. The similarities were uncanny. An ostensibly cerebral quiz like this didn't jar with the old Reithian principles of the BBC being there to "inform, educate and entertain", so it was perceived as acceptable by Aunty Beeb, and didn't offend 'outraged of Tunbridge Wells'.

There are probably only two things of any real note regarding *Top of the Form*:

- Latymer Upper School had on its team one year a teenage Hugh Grant
- The show was cancelled in 1986 because it was felt that the competitive nature of the format was at odds with contemporary "everybody's equal" thinking on education

ASK THE FAMILY

The BBC always felt that it would be immoral to give away large cash prizes, paid for with licence-payers' money, and it did still regard itself as more highbrow than ITV, and therefore superior in some way. However, seeing their commercial rival having a surprise hit with a more worthy and intellectual quiz, the BBC decided to stick its toe in the water again with another 'safe' quiz series – *Ask the Family*.

This one was very middle-class, and positively twee.

It was a hit though, especially, one suspects, in the Home Counties, and the series ran for seventeen years, from 1967 to 1984, all hosted by journalist, author and presenter Robert Robinson.

If Bamber Gascoigne, as a quiz show host, was a sort of genial but strict schoolmaster type, then Robert Robinson was very much the rather daunting cantankerous headmaster. You almost felt the contestants should be putting up their hands and calling him 'Sir'.

The show pitted two spectacularly ordinary families of four against one another in a battle of wits, general knowledge and mind-bending puzzles.

The family teams were Mum and Dad, plus two teenage children.

Again it was a knockout contest to find Britain's dullest ... er, sorry, Britain's brightest family...

Robert Robinson was famous for having arguably the worst 'comb-over' on British television.

He was fooling nobody!

There was a slightly less middle-class revival of the show in 1999 with Alan Titchmarsh in the chair. *Ask the Family* was then finally killed off in 2005 by a seriously dumbed-down, decidedly vulgar version, hosted by the poor man's Ant & Dec – Dick & Dom.

In 2018 ITV experimented with a similar format, *Britain's Brightest Family*, and made two series, hosted by Anne Hegerty, better known as a Chaser – 'The Governess'.

MASTERMIND

Each of four contestants is subjected to two minutes in the spotlight to answer questions on their chosen specialist subject, with the option to 'pass' on tricky questions.

When all four have had their turn they each return to the hotseat for two and a half minutes of questioning on general knowledge.

Keeping up their theme of worthy and intellectually cerebral quiz shows, with little to offer in terms of financial reward, the BBC continued the trend in 1972 with an original, brand-new format called *Mastermind*.

It is said that the show's creator, Bill Wright, a former RAF prisoner-of-war, was influenced by his interrogation at the hands of the Gestapo, during World War II. Hence the intimidating music and stark lighting, cold relentless questioning and general hostile atmosphere. The title of the programme's iconic signature tune says it all: 'Approaching Menace'.

Almost as famous as the ominous theme tune is the black and chrome chair, picked out in a pool of cold overhead light.

In the early years the shows were always recorded as an outside broadcast from different church or college buildings. Now it has found a home in a studio.

The original host was of course Icelandic-born journalist and writer Magnus Magnusson, who coined the perennial catchphrase "I've started so I'll finish", when the two-minute time-up buzzer caught him mid-flow.

Other presenters have hosted various twists and specialist slants on the programme, but the main replacements for Magnus, hosting the original format, have been: Peter Snow, Clive Anderson, John Humphrys, and currently, at the time of writing, Clive Myrie.

Perhaps the most memorable winner was 1980 champ, London black-cab driver Fred Housego. He was so popular with the public his impressive headline-grabbing win kick-started a lengthy media career as a celebrity in his own right, presenting on TV and hosting his own late-night radio show. He continued driving a taxi though, right through to his retirement in 2007.

A hugely successful spin-off version is *Celebrity Mastermind*, where brave celebs play for their favourite charity and risk looking very foolish, in the hope of looking brainier than viewers at home would perhaps imagine. Some achieve that goal, others do quite the opposite.

At the grand old age of fifty the show is one of the longest running quizzes on British television.

The trophy for each year's champion is a unique hand-engraved cut-glass bowl, proving that a massive cash reward isn't an essential requirement for a big hit quiz show.

SALE OF THE CENTURY

The next generation of hybrid quizzes with high-value prizes arguably started in 1971 with yet another American format, *Sale of the Century*. As with its predecessors *Dotto* and *Criss Cross Quiz*, answering general knowledge questions was a means to an end, not the complete show.

The clever built-in snag was that you got money taken away for an incorrect answer to a quiz question, so, if you spent too recklessly, there was real danger of ending up in the red, which meant you were eliminated from taking part in the rest of the show.

The original host was Nicholas Parsons, already famous as an actor, straight-man to comedian Arthur Haynes, and chairman of the long-running radio panel game *Just a Minute*. Nicholas was another no-nonsense gameshow host who took a stern schoolmasterly approach, and was more than capable of giving contestants a good ticking-off if they didn't play well.

Three contestants answered quiz questions to earn money which they could then spend on massively discounted 'sale' items in the studio.

Strategically you could buy lots of lesser items, throughout the course of the show, which you were guaranteed to take home, or you could save your money in the hope of being the week's champion who could spend their winnings on a top prize in *The Sale of the Century* at the end of the show.

Usually there was a car on offer for as little as £140.

The original ITV show always started with the famous words: "And now, from Norwich, it's the quiz of the week!"

It was made by Anglia Television in their Norwich studios. Consequently it was rather looked down upon by the major ('big five') ITV franchise holders in London and the other major cities of the UK. However, it was one of the most consistently high-rating entertainment shows of the 1970s, regularly peaking at over 20 million viewers.

Peter Marshall hosted a re-boot on Sky One from 1989 to 1991, and yet another revamp was attempted in 1997 by Challenge TV, hosted by Keith Chegwin.

Famously a complete unknown called Simon Cowell made his first television appearance as a contestant on the Sky version in 1989. He played really well. Mr Cowell perhaps foolishly turned down the chance to spend his early lead quiz winnings on a matching shawl and scarf worth £50, but he did end up winning a set of kitchen utensils worth £20. Already the go-getter!

CELEBRITY SQUARES

We have to mention *Celebrity Squares* here, if only to be able to talk about one of the UK's first truly great quintessential quizmasters, Bob Monkhouse.

Bob had already been hugely successful on radio, TV, cinema and stage as a comedian, writer, actor and presenter of shows like *Candid Camera* and *Mad Movies*. His gameshow hosting had started in 1974, with *Quick on the Draw*, featuring celebrity cartoonists. Then, famously, a year later, he became the star of the massively popular German format *The Golden Shot*, where contestants fired real crossbows all over the audience-filled studio. (It was before 'health & safety' had ever been heard of...)

Like all his many gameshows and quiz shows *Celebrity Squares* gave Bob the chance to be the comedian he was at heart, but his genial intelligence and quick-thinking made him the perfect host – handling the contestants tactfully but humorously, and steering his way around the rules of the game, whilst cleverly engaging all nine celebrity guests, without ever upstaging them. It's a tricky balancing act, but Bob was a master.

Neither of these were quizzes, as such, so they don't fall into the remit of this book. However, *Celebrity Squares*, which first aired on ITV in 1975, was one of those hybrid gameshows, which did have a quiz element, albeit tenuously. First and foremost it was a comedy game, which allowed nine witty celebrities to be used like a giant 'noughts & crosses' grid, and let their hair down, primarily for fun.

It was based on an American format called *Hollywood Squares*.

Bob Monkhouse hosted the show from 1975 to 1979, then he was invited back by ITV to front a new updated version from 1993 to 1997.

In the early years the most frequently chosen centre box was usually occupied by the erudite and spontaneously funny humorist and satirist, Willie Rushton.

The most recent series was hosted by Warwick Davis, from 2014 to 2015.

Two contestants, designated as an X or an O, chose a celebrity, based on their seating position in the nine 'noughts & crosses' boxes. Bob asked that celebrity a quiz question. They would firstly give an often cringeworthy joke answer, followed by their true guess at the answer. The contestant then had to predict whether their proper answer was correct or incorrect. If the contestant's prediction was right they won the square. If they were wrong that square went to their rival. Of course, just like *Criss Cross Quiz*, and traditional 'noughts & crosses', the idea was to win a row of three squares.

WINNER TAKES ALL

Very often TV companies had signed up top mainstream comedians of the day, and then didn't know what to do with them. Or they had their sights set on contracting a popular comedian and wanted a vehicle to attract them to their channel.

Creating scripts and sets to make comedy sketch shows was an expensive and time-consuming process, and it simply wasn't possible to fill hours of television with stand-up comedy material, so a quiz show or a gameshow was a good way to keep our funny favourites on the screen. The comedians loved it. It kept their public profile high, with a lot less work involved. They could record several quiz shows in a day, and didn't have any scripts to learn or any rehearsals to attend, yet it still gave them the opportunity to throw in a gag here and there, and even the odd witty ad lib, just to remind viewers that they still were comedians at heart. There was also a lot less risk involved – critics and viewers could be brutal about unfunny comedy shows, but a quiz wasn't going to attract that kind of scrutiny.

By 1975 jolly Jimmy Tarbuck had joined the ever-growing legion of television quiz show hosts, continuing the trend for comedians to be given the role.

In *Winner Takes All* two contestants were given 50 points each, and asked quiz questions with six possible multiple-choice answers, each one having bookie-style odds attached to it. They could gamble some of their points on their choice of answer. If they were correct they won extra points, based on the odds on offer for that particular answer.

After five questions the player with the most points went into the final. Two more contestants did the same, then the finalists played each other for £1,000.

The so-called gambling element was actually a bit of a red herring, as you were only ever going to get the odds offered for each winning answer, so it was pointless gambling based on the odds. You could only win by knowing the correct answer, and the odds for that answer were set in stone beforehand. The only real gamble was how many of your points you risked, depending how certain you were that you were right.

Winner Takes All was a highly successful ITV quiz series, devised by ex-BBC presenter Geoffrey Wheeler. He knew about quiz shows from his time on BBC's *Top of the Form*, and he had also hosted *Come Dancing* and *Songs of Praise*, which had kept him in work as a fairly earnest broadcaster. Wheeler provided the voice-overs for the series and he also wrote a lot of the questions. Eventually, when Tarbuck moved on in 1986, after twelve series, Geoffrey Wheeler took over as the host, but it only survived another two series.

The format was revived by gameshow channel, Challenge TV, in 1997, with comedian and impressionist Bobby Davro hosting. Only one series was made.

The original ITV shows were made by Yorkshire Television, who also came up with *3-2-1!* in 1978, hosted by yet another comedian – Ted Rogers. This Spanish format was pretty much unfathomable, and, as it wasn't really a quiz show, I am spared the onerous task of trying to explain it here.

Perhaps the fact that Ted's genial co-host was a humanoid dustbin says it all.

THE KRYPTON FACTOR

I need to make a quick mention here of Granada TV's *The Krypton Factor*, if only because the original host Gordon Burns always referred to it as "television's toughest quiz". It was hugely successful, running on ITV from 1977 to 1995, but the truth is that the traditional quiz element was just a couple of minutes, right at the end of the show.

In the search to find a Superman or Superwoman, Gordon Burns played Lex Luthor, throwing kryptonite-like obstacles in the way of all the earnest contestants, in the form of various tests of their super-powers. There were mental agility tests, which might involve memory or creativity; observation tests; physical tests (famously an army assault course); and in later series 'response' tests, which involved manual dexterity, even a flight simulator.

The final round was general knowledge, which was the straightforward quiz part of the show. It was a relatively short round, certainly in the context of all the other time-consuming and arduous tasks the contestants had undergone, but it was a quickfire 'fingers-on-buzzers' round, so the points could be plentiful for somebody quick-witted. This caused a bit of a controversy, because it was noted that somebody with really good general knowledge, who had lagged behind at everything else, could overtake and beat some poor soul who had excelled at mental agility and dexterity tests, and sweated their guts out, covered in mud, to come out top of the assault course round. But then, who ever said that life was fair?

A significant fact about *The Krypton Factor* is that

it was created and devised in the UK by Jeremy Fox, and was the first British gameshow format to be sold to an American TV network. The trade had all been in the opposite direction up to that point, with UK TV channels buying lots of game and quiz formats from the States.

One thing that convinces me I am right to question Gordon Burns' assertion that *The Krypton Factor* was a quiz show is the fact that some of their contestants were carried off in arnbulances with flesh wounds and fractures. In all my years on *Millionaire* I don't recall one gashed forehead or broken ankle ... The odd dented ego, yes. (Just check out Chris Evans' record on the show. He appeared twice, first time partnering Terry Wogan, then James Martin. On both occasions he and his celebrity chum reached the £10,000 question for their charities, got it wrong and plummeted to a woeful £1,000. Chris Evans was gutted the first time. The second time he actually ran off the set in shame!)

Gordon Burns hosted all 254 episodes, between 1977 and 1995, but Ben Shepherd hosted a brief revival for two series from 2009 to 2010.

Ross King hosted a couple of series of Young Krypton from 1988 to 1989.

POP QUIZ

In an effort to keep quiz shows evolving and even more appealing, experiments had been tried using celebrities as contestants, instead of ordinary working people. *Winner Takes All* made a couple of Christmas specials with celebrities answering the questions, and other TV quizzes had done the same. Of course the problem was that wealthy celebrities couldn't be seen to be winning large cash prizes for themselves, so they had to play for charity. *Celebrity Squares* had cleverly got around that dilemma, because the celebrities were purely there to help ordinary contestants win money, and of course for entertainment purposes. Gameshow *Blankety-Blank* used celebrities in a similar way.

As far back as the 1950s the BBC had employed celebrities to play amusing TV panel games, where there were no cash prizes involved, just the glory and sometimes ruthless one-upmanship of winning – shows like *What's My Line* and *Twenty Questions*.

However, these weren't quiz shows, but, in 1981, DJ Mike Read began hosting a celebrity quiz on BBC One – *Pop Quiz*.

DJ Mike Read had already established himself as a professor of pop, being one of the co-founders and first compilers of *The Guinness Book of Hit Singles*, the bible of popular music.

Mike Read, just back from Mullets R Us

Two teams of three pop stars (occasionally celebrity pop fans or DJs) competed against one another, answering questions on pop music. It was a simple enough idea, but it attracted some of the real top music legends of that period – George Michael, Phil Collins, Roger Taylor (from Queen), Meatloaf, Bob Geldof and Robert Plant all made appearances on the teams.

It has to be said, at that time, I wasn't taking quiz shows too seriously. In fact, I wrote a whole series of daily sketches for Chris Tarrant on Capital Radio, under the umbrella title, 'Game for a Cringe', where we unmercifully spoofed quiz and gameshows, and took the proverbial out of the more smarmy self-serving hosts.

Chris did do competitions on his daily radio show and listeners could win money or prizes, but very often he didn't take that terribly seriously either. I remember one game he played where listeners had to phone in and identify popular songs, which were gargled by one of his assistants in the studio. Yes – you did read right – gargled! Chris used to get a right old soaking, sitting next to her, but it was very funny.

However, by the end of the eighties, Chris had been tempted over to the dark side, and was himself hosting proper quiz and gameshows. Actually, it wasn't a dark side at all. He loved every minute of it.

Chronologically we aren't quite there yet, but I mention that here as Chris successfully hosted a revival of *Pop Quiz* in 1994.

BULLSEYE

Bullseye is a perfect example of a hybrid quiz/gameshow. In order to keep quizzes visually exciting ITV were again experimenting with merging questions and answers with sports or traditional games. In 1981 they launched *Bullseye*, a quiz based on the centuries-old pub game, darts. The show involved pairs of contestants working as a team – a good darts player, and a partner who was hopefully good at general knowledge, ie: a thrower and a knower. Both had to be good. The accuracy of the darts determined how much money was won, and a wrongly-placed dart could forfeit your team's turn. The 'knower' had to get the quiz questions right to actually secure any prize at all. Wrongly answered questions could lead to another 'knower' stealing the money.

The basic idea was arrived at quite academically by Andrew Wood, a man who had been studying and researching what elements make for a good TV gameshow. He was helped to flesh the format out by veteran comedian Norman Vaughan (former host of The Golden Shot), who, presumably, was hoping to front the show. In the end the star role was given to a man 14 years younger, Jim Bowen, a Northern club comic who had made a name for himself as a popular regular on ITV's big hit series *The Comedians*.

Show creator Andrew Wood had learned that people seem to love sport and gambling, so he'd added a gambling element in the end-game. The winning duo had to decide whether to risk everything they'd won so far for a chance to play for that night's mystery star prize. Both contestants now had to throw darts to get a combined score of 101 or more. If they achieved that then they won the star prize, plus everything else they'd accumulated in the earlier rounds. However, if they failed, they lost everything and went home with nothing but their 'BFH', as Jim used to say, 'bus fare home'. The added torture for a losing pair was that Jim would insist on taking them to look at the reveal of that night's mystery star prize, regardless: "Look at what you could have won!"

The star prize could be a car, but it could also be a pricey white elephant. What were two ordinary working blokes from the middle of Bradford going to do with a speedboat? The famous consolation prize was 'Bully' – a bendy toy bull, the mascot of the show. In many ways that collectible and endearing trophy was more appealing, and more use than a speedboat.

Jim Bowen played the part of a lovable bumbling buffoon. Revelling in his own mistakes and faux pas, he almost deliberately went out of his way to be the very antithesis of the super-slick gameshow host. In fact he was no fool, and had been a deputy headteacher before he found his way into comedy. His co-host was a professional darts player, Tony Green, who acted as scorekeeper, genial referee and helpful cheerleader for the 'throwers'.

The show was hugely successful and got massive

viewing figures for nearly fifteen years, ending in 1995. A revival of the show was launched on Challenge TV, back in 2006, this time hosted by Dave Spikey, another (younger) northern club comic. Tony Green was still there, but the reboot wasn't as successful as the original, and only ran for one lengthy series.

Bullseye is so well-loved as a brand that it has prominently featured three times in ITV's occasional compendiums of gameshows:

Ant & Dec's Gameshow Marathon in 2005

Vernon Kay's Gameshow Marathon in 2007

And, having just been voted one of the country's five favourite gameshows of all time, *Alan Carr's Epic Gameshow* in 2020.

In 1991 the BBC created a similar pub game/quiz hybrid, combining general knowledge questions with snooker, under the title *Big Break*. The comedian host was Jim Davidson and the snooker professional co-host was John Virgo. It was another massive hit, and ran, on and off, for over twenty years.

BLOCKBUSTERS

Blockbusters must be one of the most revived and reinvented quiz shows on British TV. It has appeared on five different channels, with six different hosts.

The original series was adapted from an American format of the same name, and was first seen on ITV in 1983, hosted by the avuncular Bob Holness. The major difference with the British version was that the contestants were teenagers. In America it was adults who competed.

One strange, and slightly controversial, departure from the quiz show norm was that one player was somewhat unfairly competing against two others playing together. It was never really explained why this was, but nobody seemed to complain. We have seen earlier that life on TV is rarely fair.

The basic idea was to traverse across or down a honeycomb-style grid, in an uninterrupted series of connections, by answering quiz questions. Each 'honeycomb' hexagon contained a letter, which was the first letter of the answer to the question. The single player had to link hexagons vertically, without being blocked by the duo, who were trying to link hexagons horizontally.

The winner of the match (just one of them if it was the duo) then went on to play the end-game – the Gold Run. The idea here was to get all the way across the grid from left to right, but a wrong answer turned the hexagon black and blocked your path.

Bob Holness, one of the nicest men on British television, hosted ten series on ITV, from 1983 to 1993. He also hosted two series when it transferred to Sky One in 1994 and 1995. In both 1987 and 1988 readers of the *TV Times* voted *Blockbusters* the most popular quiz on television.

Never mind all that commercial success – it would have been worth mounting the whole series just to hear contestants say, "Could I have a 'P' please, Bob?"

Further incarnations of *Blockbusters*,
after it was axed by ITV:

Bob Holness for Sky TV – 1994 to 1995

Michael Aspel for BBC2 – 1997

Liza Tarbuck for Sky TV – 2000 to 2001

Vernon Kay for ITV's Gameshow Marathon – 2007

Simon Mayo for Challenge TV – 2012

Dara O'Briain for Comedy Central – 2019

BOB'S FULL HOUSE

By the 1980s the BBC had been forced by market pressures to succumb to mass-appeal programmes, even if they weren't quite as worthy and 'Reithian' as they once had been. It was open warfare between ITV and the BBC for ratings.

Bob's Full House was a BBC quiz programme, based loosely around the age-old game of bingo. That sounds pretty downmarket, and dumbed-down by even the most extreme gameshow standards, but it was kept classy by the presence of the genial host, quick quizmaster and sartorially-immaculate bingo-caller, Bob Monkhouse.

Around that time there had been a bidding war for the major entertainment and comedy stars of the period. Many of the top names swapped channels, lured by massive fees, and promises of wonderful shows. Bruce Forsyth had started his television career on ITV, then moved to the BBC to host *The Generation Game*, but was lured back to ITV again in 1978 with a large cash incentive and the ego-boosting offer of *Bruce Forsyth's Big Night*, which gave him virtually the whole of ITV primetime on Saturday evenings, to do with what he wanted. In the end that proved to be a disaster, but Brucie remained at ITV for many years, mainly hosting gameshows. Top comedy impressionist Mike Yarwood jumped ship from the BBC to ITV in 1982, and even the BBC's golden boys Morecambe & Wise had emigrated to the opposition in 1978.

The BBC were haemorrhaging talent fast, but the traffic wasn't all one-way. They had managed to sign Bob

Monkhouse for an exclusive three-year deal, the main attraction of which (apart from the money of course) was the fact they were offering him a series of comedy chat shows, simply entitled *The Bob Monkhouse Show*. This was Bob's dream, to host a show all about his beloved comedy, and have the opportunity to introduce talented new comedians to the small screen, as well as giving him an excuse to welcome some of his peers for an hilarious conversation – Tommy Cooper, Spike Milligan, Les Dawson, Norman Wisdom, Frankie Howerd, Victoria Wood, Bob Hope, etc. It should be noted though that Bob, through his chat show, was the first to introduce us to American comedy greats, like Joan Rivers, Robin Williams (as a stand-up), Steven Wright, Emo Phillips, Rita Rudner, and a then young and unknown Jim Carrey. That was the icing on the cake for Bob, but he was also contracted to host game and quiz shows for the BBC as well. Let's face it, he had already proved himself to be the grand master of the genre, over on ITV, with the likes of *The Golden Shot*, *Celebrity Squares* and *Family Fortunes*.

So, in 1984, Bob, stylishly and with his highly-intelligent tongue very firmly in his cheek, dragged the BBC, kicking and screaming, into the bingo-calling world of "Twenty-two – two little ducks" and "All the fours – droopy drawers".

As in any bingo game the aim was to fill your number card, but you had to answer quiz questions to do that. Bob had plenty of opportunities to ad lib and make wise cracks about the contestants during the gameplay, but he had also insisted on having an opening comedy monologue, where he could showcase his prodigious talent as a stand-up comedian and gag-teller.

Despite the fact that the financial rewards were great, the big worry for those comedians, when they became prolific gameshow hosts, was that the public would forget that they were, first and foremost, entertainers from a much-loved variety theatre tradition. Bruce Forsyth once summed it up in an interview in 2005, when he was asked if he had any regrets in his life, and he wistfully answered, "Yes. I did too many gameshows". A lot of people had forgotten, or maybe never even knew, that he was probably Britain's finest ever all-round entertainer. He could do comedy and impressions, he could dance beautifully, he was a superb jazz pianist, he was a master at audience participation, and he had a terrific singing voice. I saw his two-hour live one-man (and an orchestra) theatre show on two separate occasions, and it was a brilliant masterclass in quality entertainment. One of the most memorable stage shows I have ever seen. No support acts, just a maestro commanding a splendid variety show single-handedly.

There was one rather strange rule in *Bob's Full House*, whereby a contestant who answered a question wrong was "wallied", which meant losing their turn. Openly calling them a wally, in front of 15 million viewers, seems a little harsh, particularly in this woke day and age. The dictionary definition of a wally being someone who is stupid or foolish. In all his years on *Millionaire* Chris Tarrant never once called anyone stupid ... although I do know there were times when he was sorely tempted...

The idea of a TV bingo quiz was revisited several times after Bob's Full House, with different titles and different hosts:

One to Win – Andrew O'Connor (BBC)

Lucky Numbers – Shane Richie (ITV)

The Biggest Game in Town – Steve le Fevre (ITV)

ODD ONE OUT

During the 1980s the BBC were having to become increasingly more competitive with the growing number of commercial channels, so they had to adapt to be less squeamish about gameshows and quiz shows, which meant more and more started to filter their way through the corporation and on to our screens.

Odd One Out was one such quiz series, loosely based on an American format called *Knockout*. It used that tried and tested TV gameshow staple, just like it said on the tin, finding the odd one out from a list of four words or phrases. For a bonus point you could answer why it was the odd one out – in other words, how the other three were connected.

In 1982 magician Paul Daniels was given the job of hosting the show, which was a very smart move on the part of BBC executives, as he turned out to make a good quizmaster, and it kept one of their top stars on our screens, without the need to come up with a whole new batch of expensive magic tricks.

Paul Daniels was one of the BBC's top entertainers at that time, with his spectacular Saturday night TV series *The Paul Daniels Magic Show* at the peak of its powers. Daniels, an extremely intelligent, amiable and sharp-witted performer, made a great host for a quiz series.

EVERY SECOND COUNTS

In 1985 astrologer Russell Grant made an untransmitted BBC pilot of an American quiz format called *Every Second Counts*. The show was commissioned as a series, but the host was replaced by magician Paul Daniels. You would have thought an astrologer would have seen that one coming...

Once again it played to Daniels' strengths as a quizmaster, as well as his ability to ad lib and gently tease the contestants, learned over many years performing comedy magic round the northern club circuit, and, without getting thumped, pulling sometimes reluctant volunteers up on stage from the audience.

> Three married couples competed in a quiz to win vital seconds of time. The couple with the highest number of seconds used that time in the final round to answer quiz questions, against the clock, for increasingly valuable prizes.

Every Second Counts was so well-received it ran for nine series between 1986 and 1993, establishing Paul as one of TV's most successful quiz show hosts in the UK.

I always felt Paul Daniels got a raw deal with the British tabloid press, and the media generally. I never quite understood why. They seem to single out certain people for harsher criticism and treatment than perhaps they deserve. Jeremy Beadle was always another. With poor old 'Beadlebum' it was probably slightly more understandable, as he'd made his name by playing pranks on people, so I suppose he was wrongly perceived as a bit cruel or unkind. In fact, it's estimated he raised over £100 million for charity in his relatively short life. Daniels didn't have that millstone of perceived cruelty though, so what was their problem with him? Perhaps it was Paul's super-confident brash approach to performing, which can be frowned upon in good ol' timid 'know-your-place' Blighty. Or maybe there was a hint of envy. The green-eyed monster rearing its ugly head among ageing male journalists. A short balding Yorkshireman having a much younger beautiful woman by his side ... How dare he flaunt his good fortune!

And, speaking of 'balding', Paul readily admitted that he wore a wig in his early days of playing northern nightclubs, to try to look younger. He also readily admitted that it became ridiculous and in fact unnecessary, so he stopped wearing it quite early on in his television career, and 'came out' about his thinning hairline. He never wore a hairpiece again. For years afterwards the wig jokes and jibes continued, however, with his Spitting Image puppet still portraying him in a comedy spinning wig several years after he'd thrown his real one away. Let's not forget this wasn't coming from some lazy comic doing the same tired old gags every night, this was from a TV show which boasted of its topical and up-to-the-minute satire. Hmmm...

In 2001 softly-softly investigative journalist Louis Theroux went on the trail of some of our weird and wonderful crackpot celebrities, hoping to expose and mock their personality flaws and imperfections. The BBC Two series was called *When Louis Met...*

His wily, some might say sneaky, and deceivingly low-key approach, did come as near as anybody got to making Jimmy Savile's mask slip momentarily, giving us the first public glimpse of Savile's very dark side, but others were less deserving of his cunningly calculated approach. Other weird celebrities Louis tried to gently mock included eccentrics like Chris Eubank and Ann Widdecombe, and, strangely in my view, Paul and Debbie Daniels. I'm sure he was hoping to expose a gold-digger and a seedy older man. In fact what he did uncover was a very happy, quite ordinary loving couple, who adored one another, and made each other laugh. Shock horror!

I only once worked with Paul Daniels – strangely not doing magic or a quiz – but with him in a presenter role on the big, lavish (infamous!) Royal Family version of *It's a Knockout* from Alton Towers. I had been warned that Paul could be difficult and didn't suffer fools. I have heard that expression used a lot about big-name stars, but I have always believed that no performer should ever have to suffer fools. It's them that are up there with egg on their face if a 'fool' behind the scenes has not prepared the show properly. All I can say is that, when he arrived, I found Paul Daniels one of the most delightful, considerate, warm, funny, intelligent, professional, kind, friendly stars I have ever had the pleasure of working with. And he had one of the sharpest brains of anybody I've ever met. As they say in my home county of Yorkshire, "I speak as I find!"

So what's that got to do with quiz shows? I hear you ask. Well, he became a very proficient quiz show host, and I don't think he always gets the credit he deserves in the history of British television. And he was an exceptionally good magician … Just saying…

ULTRA QUIZ

In episode one a massive number of contestants was quickly whittled down to a more manageable number with a simple elimination quiz. The remaining players were then taken to a new location where they endured physical challenges as well as more demanding quiz questions to keep reducing their number. The idea was, by the end of the series, they had eliminated everybody except one champion who would take home the then record-breaking cash prize of £10,000.

In the early 1980s ITV was still cash-rich. The explosion of cable and satellite channels hadn't yet happened, so they still eagerly grabbed the lion's share of the media advertising revenue in the UK. It was inevitable then that they would want to get bigger and better with their quizzes by throwing money at them, to outdo the BBC, who had now started to take ITV on at their own quiz game.

Ultra Quiz, as the name suggests, was meant to be the biggest and brashest quiz show ever, broadening its horizons well beyond the cosy safety of a TV studio. It was, unusually, a format purchased from Japanese TV. Japanese game show formats were usually considered too extreme for sensitive British eyes. Remember the glee with which Clive James, then Chris Tarrant, showed us stomach-churning excerpts from the Japanese 'torture game show', *Endurance*? We watched through our fingers, shocked, but amused by the contestants' willingness to be terrified, beaten, electrocuted, half-drowned and humiliated, all in the name of entertainment. It was reassuring to know that this sort of programming could never happen in dear Old Blighty. They were forced to do horrendous things like sticking their head into a box of cockroaches, or eating a kangaroo's penis ... Yes, yes, I know. We succumbed eventually and cuddly Ant & Dec started torturing people in the Australian jungle in much the same way. The good thing was, I suppose, that they were only torturing 'celebrities'.

I worked with Chris for many gloriously funny years on *Tarrant on TV*, taking the mickey out of outrageous foreign shows like *Endurance*, but it really had to come to an end in 2006, when we realised we could no longer take the moral high ground when it came to international TV. The whole series was based on laughing at how other countries went to disgustingly extreme lengths to grab viewers, but, by that time, we could no longer point the finger. We were every bit as guilty.

Anyway – back to *Ultra Quiz*. Even that had torture elements in its native Japanese outings. Contestants were given horrible forfeits or unpleasant booby prizes if they lost. They could be thrown into jail, or off a ship, or be forced to eat something unpalatable. Genial ITV couldn't go that far (at that time!), but there was still a cruel element to the way contestants were callously dropped and eliminated, being sent off unceremoniously with nothing more than their fare home. The watered-down version was adapted for UK television by programme consultant

Jeremy Beadle, although he never got to host the show. In series one Michael Aspel hosted remotely from a London studio. Sally James and the now-disgraced Jonathan King were his roving co-hosts, on the ground. Two thousand people turned up on Brighton beach to take part in episode one, and were mercilessly reduced to 200 with a simple true or false elimination quiz. The survivors were herded on to a train, then a cross-channel ferry to France, where there was a much tougher quiz to answer, and more contestants were shooed off home in ignominy.

Every episode meant a new exotic location, including Holland, Bahrain and Hong Kong. In the studio Aspel was flanked by astrologer Russell Grant and computer expert David Manuel, who were there to accurately forecast and predict who would win. Not too surprisingly, they both got it wrong.

Ultra Quiz had mixed success, although there were three series made in all, in 1983, 1984 and 1985. It seems though that ITV's faith diminished with each series and the budget was reduced year on year. The studio element was dropped after series one, and the far-sighted forecasters were suddenly absent, due, presumably, to unforeseen circumstances.

David Frost and Willie Rushton hosted the second globe-trotting series, bringing a certain gravitas to the proceedings, but, by series three, the hosts were Stu Francis and Sara Hollamby, and the contestants got no further than Bournemouth Pier.

GOING FOR GOLD

Going for Gold was one of the first shows to be 'stripped' across the whole week on daytime TV, from Monday through Friday. It was a simple general knowledge elimination quiz with each daily show providing a winner who automatically went into Friday's final. The losers came back the next day to fight again, with a replacement contestant. The weekly winners then moved on to semi-finals, with a grand final determining the series champion.

With the advent of wall-to-wall daytime television the BBC had more hours to fill and so budgets had to be spread thinner. Quizzes were relatively low-cost, high-output programming, so they became ever more prevalent on the Beeb.

The pressure was mounting for bigger and better quizzes, but budget was always going to be a problem, especially for the BBC. Their solution, in 1987, was to mount an international (well, partial-European) quiz contest called *Going for Gold*. The other competing countries contributed financially, which meant, particularly by daytime television standards, that the budget was higher than normal, consequently production values could be glossier and more impressive.

Playing host we stacked the odds in our favour as four of the seven competing nations were always England, Scotland, Wales and Northern Ireland. Not only that but the show was hosted in England by Henry Kelly, in a strong Irish accent, so contestants for whom English was a second language had a somewhat unfair disadvantage.

Despite everything being clearly weighted in favour of those on home turf, out of nine Euro series, there were only two English champions, one Welsh one, and not a single victor from Scotland or Ireland.

One funny story I heard about *Going for Gold* was told to me by a close friend of mine, comedian Ray Turner, who was paid to 'warm up' the audiences for the show. Because the budget was still quite frugal the studio wasn't large, so audiences were pretty small anyway, but one particular day a large coach party, who were supposed to be attending, cancelled for some reason, so Ray had ONE man in the audience to entertain that day. He decided, as any true professional would, that he would do his job anyway, and Ray gave this chap the full works, including handing him a ticket for a daily raffle that was drawn to keep the audiences engaged and smiling. When Ray, pausing for dramatic effect and building up the dramatic tension, announced the raffle winner, the man excitedly jumped and shouted in a surprised voice, "It's me!"

Unfortunately, part way through the recording, the man said he had somewhere else to be and got up and left...

> With the traditional lazy linguistic attitudes of the UK, participants were only invited from English-speaking European nations, so the French weren't welcome.

FIFTEEN TO ONE

Fifteen contestants, each behind a lectern, were given three lives, which could be lost by either getting a general knowledge question wrong or answering too slowly. After losing their third life they were history. The number of contestants reduced until three were left standing, to play in the end-game to find the show winner. After fifteen shows there were fifteen winners who competed in the grand final to find the series champion.

Channel 4 jumped on the quiz bandwagon in 1988 with *Fifteen to One*, often referred to, at that time, as the toughest quiz show on television. Of course Channel 4 had successfully screened the letters-and-numbers game *Countdown* since they first launched in 1982, but that wasn't a general knowledge quiz.

Instead of going down the chirpy comedian or genial personality route to find a host for *Fifteen to One*, Channel 4 opted for veteran TV producer William G Stewart, a man steeped in television, but not usually in front of the camera. He came across as highly efficient, dapper and professional, but with all the easy wit, back-slapping bonhomie and avuncular charm of a haemorrhoidal income tax inspector. There was no humorous banter with the contestants and little consolation or sympathy when they were eliminated.

William G Stewart remained as host for fifteen years, then the show was given a ten-year break. It returned to Channel 4 in 2014, this time fronted by political activist and broadcaster Sandi Toksvig, another host not exactly renowned for her cosy, cuddly geniality and warmth. There were also occasional celebrity specials hosted by Adam Hills.

EVERYBODY'S EQUAL

The idea of a large number of contestants being ruthlessly reduced to one champion was taken to the next level in 1989 with ITV's *Everybody's Equal*. In this series the entire studio audience of 200 people were given electronic keypads, so that they could all answer every question. Of course advances in TV technology were driving these kind of shows. A few years earlier and it wouldn't have been possible for the whole audience to take part.

It gave a fresh-faced Chris Tarrant another opportunity to hone his quiz hosting skills, a man who was destined to become perhaps the UK's ultimate quizmaster.

In many ways *Everybody's Equal* paved the way for his opus magnum, *Who Wants to Be a Millionaire?* It was made by the same production company, Celador Productions, who were evolving along with Chris, and quickly learning how to make rivetingly addictive must-see quizzes.

Forming a relationship with Chris, Celador were also experimenting with the new emerging technology and realising the value of multiple-choice questions with four possible answers displayed. The answer was right there for all to see, but which one was it? This made for a great 'play-at-home' factor. In my opinion that was one of the key elements which made *Millionaire* such a huge success. Even up to the million-pound question the correct answer was staring at us all, right there, up on the screen. Even just a random guess had a 25% chance of being right.

The *Everybody's Equal* technology also allowed the show producers to assess the speed with which audience members were answering questions, which would eventually lead to the *Fastest Finger First* selection round in *Millionaire*.

One of the enjoyable things about *Everybody's Equal* was that if just one person in the audience got a relatively easy question wrong (which did happen), or chose a stupid answer, Chris could be told who that person was and tease them unmercifully. That naming and shaming tactic could end up being cruel in the hands of some hosts, but Chris has an unerring knack of being able to gently rib people, in an amusing way, without them taking offence. It's a rare skill.

Internal ITV politics put an end to *Everybody's Equal* after just two series, but it had sowed the seed for what was to become the most successful TV quiz show in the world. The seminal *Everybody's Equal* format was recycled however by Channel 5 in 1997, as *Whittle*, with comedian Tim Vine as the host.

$64,000 QUESTION

This classic and once-pioneering American format was given another British airing in 1990. Strangely, despite the very impressive, expensive-looking set and some nice bells and whistles, it didn't make a particularly successful or gripping quiz series, but it is worth mentioning for a number of reasons.

- It was hosted by the man who was still king of the quiz show, back then, Bob Monkhouse.
- It boasted the highest cash prize ever offered on a UK TV quiz show, at that time. That ceiling kept rising, with the grudging blessing of the ITV governing body, the IBA, who were constantly having to succumb to market pressure.
- It was the American format which, thirty-five years earlier, had influenced British TV's first ever proper general knowledge quiz show, Double Your Money.

The downside on British TV was that, despite sticking with the eye-catching American title, the top prize was nowhere near $64,000. At that time the top cash prize allowed in the UK was £6,000. Special permission had to be sought from the IBA to up this slightly to £6,400, just to make the doubling-up of the cash work. Nevertheless, it was still a tiny fraction of the promised $64,000.

I know one of the masterminds behind this and many other UK quiz shows, top TV executive and gameshow

Presumably *Ultra Quiz* got away with giving a grand prize of £10,000 in the final week because it was an accumulated jackpot, amassed over many episodes where no money was given away.

guru, Stephen Leahy. I can well imagine that there was a lot of noisy and active lobbying to the IBA to get their blessing to give away the equivalent of $64,000, but the IBA weren't renowned for being terribly flexible. In fairness to them I suppose it was in their remit not to be easily badgered into making rash or controversial decisions.

The other downside of this new incarnation of *$64,000 Question* was that the format didn't really allow Bob to play to his strengths as a comedian either.

Even Bob's undoubted quiz hosting expertise failed to deliver much in the way of tension or drama. Perhaps it was all a bit too safe, with too little jeopardy. There were two cosy cash safety nets for contestants, which meant they could still go home with quite a bit of money, even if they failed to get the top prize. By that point audiences were starting to enjoy the *Ultra Quiz/Everybody's Equal* gladiatorial brutality of sending losers home with absolutely nothing.

Nevertheless, thanks I'm sure to Monkhouse's safe pair of hands, not to mention his perennial popularity, ITV did run *$64,000 Question* for four series, ending in 1993.

Of course the key ingredient of the money for the next question doubling was about to be taken to new dizzy heights with *Who Wants to Be a Millionaire?*

WIPEOUT

We're almost getting to the point in UK television history where there is such a proliferation of quiz shows, as daytime TV explodes, that I can't possibly mention them all. However, *Wipeout* has several interesting factors.

Based on an American format with the same name, it started in 1994 on BBC One in primetime, hosted by now-established quizmaster Paul Daniels. It ran for four series, until 1996. There was then a two-year hiatus, but it did return to BBC One in 1998 with a new host – Bob Monkhouse.

This time, however, Bob's version of the quiz was shown on daytime television.

This transfer to daytime meant a drastic budget reduction and subsequent loss of high production values. It was Bob's only venture into daytime television on weekdays, and he continued prolifically making *Wipeout* recordings almost up to his tragic and untimely death in 2003.

The reduction in budget meant they couldn't afford to have a live audience in the studio, but Bob was such a master of his comedy craft that he could still play perfectly-timed jokes and ad libs out to a silent imaginary crowd, instinctively knowing exactly how long to leave for a dubbed laugh that would be added on to the soundtrack during the post-production process. If you watch a Monkhouse episode of *Wipeout* it's hard to believe that the lively responsive audience wasn't actually there. The man was a genius.

The questions were more like pub quiz trivia than general knowledge.

Wipeout, being on the BBC, couldn't really offer massive cash prizes. In the Paul Daniels prime-time version there were some reasonably decent prizes of goods and services, but the daytime budget meant that Bob was giving away even less.

NUMBER ONE HITS IN 1966

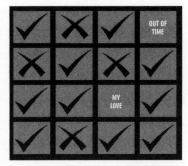

Three contestants faced a grid of twelve or sixteen squares, each square displaying a right or wrong answer to one question. (For example – sixteen song titles, with the question "Number one hits in 1966". Eleven of the songs had been 1966 Number Ones, and five hadn't.) The object obviously was to win money by only choosing squares showing correct answers. Choosing a square with a wrong answer wiped out all the money you'd made so far. Good fun to watch, but brutal to play!

WHO WANTS TO BE A MILLIONAIRE?

And then there was *Millionaire*…

It is no exaggeration to say that *Who Wants to Be a Millionaire?* changed the face of quiz shows for ever – and not just here in the UK, but all around the world. Even though it had familiar tried-and-tested elements within its format, it didn't look like any other gameshow before it, and it felt modern, fresh and made must-see compulsive viewing.

The genesis of the show is interesting, and what you are about to read is straight from the horse's mouth. The initial idea came from a man called David Briggs, who I interviewed at length for this book.

I've known David for a very long time, as he was an executive producer at Capital Radio when Chris Tarrant was hosting their hugely successful breakfast show, for which I supplied comedy scripts and strand ideas on a daily basis. David was very hands-on with any new content for Chris's show, which was taking the Greater London airwaves by storm every morning. He was also very good at attracting sponsors to finance certain strands. David was great to work for, as he recognised a good idea, and he was happy to use that sponsorship money to pay a fair rate for my input. He was keen to make a move into television, so he left Capital in 1993 to join breakfast broadcasters, GMTV, as Marketing Manager. Fundamentally they wanted him to make money for them, something he was good at doing, but he found it stifling as it mainly involved creating those daily phone-in competitions, with ridiculously easy questions: "What is a poodle? A – a religious book, B – an orange fruit, or C – a dog?"

Of course, thousands of viewers immediately thought, "Wow! I know that one!" and phoned in for a chance to win the cash prize. David told me that the job wasn't creatively stimulating, for obvious reasons, and he didn't end up staying too long.

However, it had given him an idea, which was to end up making his fortune. The people who phoned in to those mind-numbingly simple competitions had to pay a pound on a premium rate phone line to enter, and David soon spotted that those calls were generating huge amounts of cash, which paid for the prize, and then some. He realised that here was a way of bringing in enough money to offer a colossal cash prize, that no previous TV gameshow had ever been able to afford. Perhaps even as much as a million pounds. As David told me – a million is a magical number. So, contrary to received wisdom, what came first was the prize. Not everybody was going to win a million, but the very real chance could be there. So the next big question was: what were they going to have to do to win a million pounds?

David had been very clever at devising phone-in competitions and interactive games to involve and engage the legions of listeners when he was overseeing Chris Tarrant's breakfast show on Capital FM. Thanks to the runaway success of Chris's show the station was raking in huge amounts of advertising revenue, so David could afford to offer reasonably generous prizes. One of the most gripping games he devised for Chris was a strand

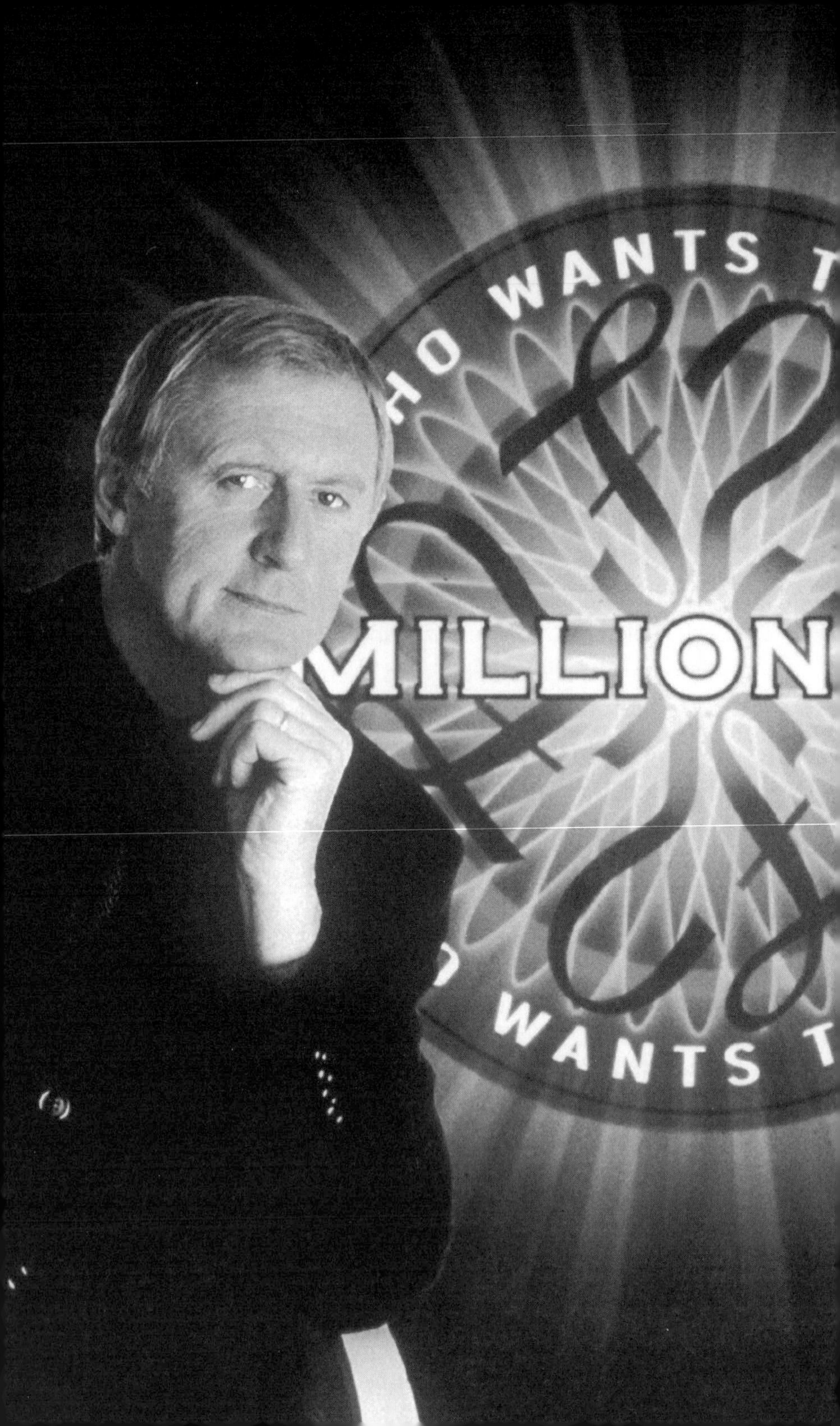

HO WANTS T
MILLION
O WANTS T

called *Double or Quits*, where callers answered quiz questions for ever-increasing cash prizes. The first correct answer won them just a pound, but the next question was for two pounds, and so on. It's amazing how quickly the money escalated when it was doubled like that every time. As they say in America, "Do the math!" Answer just fifteen questions correctly and you've already gone from a quid to over £16,000! Within a few minutes people could be playing for serious cash sums. Chris said that the management at Capital Radio were getting nervous that the game could bankrupt the company, because, theoretically, there was no top limit to the prize pot.

The company coffers were perfectly safe, however, because there was a significant factor which stopped even the smartest high rollers in their tracks. The jeopardy was that a wrong answer meant you lost every penny you'd won so far, and you were history. Very few people were willing to risk a decent amount of money they'd already amassed, unless they were absolutely certain of the next answer, and 100% certainty is an extremely tough call, especially when a lot of hard cash is at stake. That clever gameplay feature, of course, has been at the heart of many quiz shows, right from *Double Your Money* and *$64 Question*. David and Chris realised though that they could create real drama by pushing callers to breaking point, and goading them into a sweat-inducing state of indecision over giving up or carrying on. These were emotionally-charged difficult decisions being made by real people, live on radio. The game was a huge success, with callers clamouring to take part.

This had taught David that we all have a range of

knowledge, but human frailty says that we become less and less confident of the accuracy of that knowledge as the stakes become higher and higher. Here was a dramatic way of offering a possible prize of a million pounds. David scribbled a two-page document, roughly sketching out this idea, whereby answering perhaps twenty general knowledge questions correctly would lead to a million-pound jackpot.

When David left Capital Radio to move into television he and Chris Tarrant had remained good friends, so Chris was David's first thought for hosting such a show. At that stage he had given his programme idea the working title of *Cash Mountain*. Chris told David that if he received any interest in his idea he would host a pilot show for him, to help get the format off the ground, although Chris admits that he thought the title *Cash Mountain* was a bit 'naff'.

David Briggs didn't have too many contacts in television, so he took the idea to show two old mates from his Capital Radio days – Steve Knight and Mike Whitehill. Steve had been a copywriter in the advertising department and Mike had been one of the station's press officers. Like David they had left radio and they had, at that time, become a successful duo of TV comedy scriptwriters and show creators, under contract to Celador Productions.

Steve Knight, now better known as Steven Knight, is an internationally successful film and TV screenwriter, probably most famous for creating and writing BBC's long-running drama, *Peaky Blinders*.

Steve and Mike were intrigued by the idea behind *Cash Mountain*, and showed it to the television production company's CEO, Paul Smith. This started a series of happy coincidences, because Celador Productions had enjoyed working with Chris Tarrant, hosting their show *Everybody's Equal*, so Paul Smith was keen to find a new vehicle for Chris's talents as a quizmaster.

Just like Steve and Mike, Paul Smith could see the potential of the basic notion of *Cash Mountain*, and knew that Chris would make the perfect host, but he felt it needed some interesting embellishments. He sent David away to work with Steve and Mike to polish, hone and enhance the basic format. That's when they came up with the key ingredient of the lifelines, which are now synonymous with *Millionaire*, and spawned many of Chris's oft-quoted catchphrases for the show.

> It was in fact David Briggs, during a dry run of the show, who came up with one of the most iconic catchphrases. He told Chris they needed a definite moment of commitment from a contestant, so he suggested simply asking "Is that your final answer?"

The original three iconic lifelines were of course: Phone a Friend; 50–50; and Ask the Audience. Other lifelines have been added since, some not lasting long. 'Switch' was tried towards the end of Chris Tarrant's tenure on the show, where the question could be discarded and swapped for a brand new one. That has now been dropped for the Clarkson era, and replaced by Ask the Host. I know for a fact that Chris's conscience wouldn't have let him agree to that one. He's actually very bright and knowledgeable, but he just couldn't have lived with the guilt of possibly slipping up and losing somebody their hard-earned winnings.

Celador organised several office run-throughs of the quiz, to perfect the format and iron out any teething problems. Fastest Finger First, all the lifelines and the gameplay were tried and tested before it was pitched to a broadcaster, but the title was still *Cash Mountain* at this stage. Paul Smith took the fully-formed show to ITV, brimming with confidence.

The first ITV executive he approached, who had better remain anonymous, turned it down, with the classic put-down, "I'm sorry, but cash reward shows are dead." If that sounds uncannily familiar you are probably, like me, reminded of the infamous shoot-me-now quote by a Decca Records executive to an unknown group called The Beatles, back in 1962. He said, "Guitar groups are on the way out." On that shaky premise he famously turned The Beatles down, allowing George Martin at EMI to step in and snap them up. Oops!

(Take heart anybody who has been temporarily crushed by rejection!)

Channel 4 also rejected the idea, and the BBC were never even going to consider anything so mercenary. In any case their idea of a *Cash Mountain* would have been a couple of grand and a cuddly toy, and that wasn't going to set the world on fire. At heart there was no doubt this was an ITV show. All of which meant that the whole project ground to a bit of a standstill.

Paul Smith kept the faith, however, and clung on to the idea, biding his time. David Briggs told me that there was always a tremendously positive attitude throughout Celador that said, "We are going to make this happen!"

Time passes, as do ITV chiefs, so Paul Smith re-pitched the idea. The next wave of incoming ITV executives were more far-sighted and encouraging, and started showing signs of genuine interest. The ITV Director of Programmes at that time, David Liddiment, had one niggling concern, however, just like the bosses back at Capital Radio. He was worried that every contestant would walk away with shed-loads of money, potentially bankrupting the programme. He was particularly nervous that they were giving too much help to the contestants by putting the correct answers up there on the screen. There was only one way to convince him. Paul Smith and David Briggs let Liddiment play the game, using his office staff for Ask the Audience and Phone a Friend lifelines. It was too easy though just to let him play for imaginary money, which he'd feel free to gamble recklessly, so they asked him to open his wallet and play for real money. Every penny he was carrying was on the line. Of course, as soon as his uncertainties kicked in about his answers to the questions, and his own hard-earned cash was suddenly at risk, he realised that his worries were unfounded. Liddiment admitted that by question two he was already sold! He could now see just how clever the game mechanics really were.

Claudia Rosencrantz, ITV's Controller of Entertainment at the time, loved the show, but hated the title. The name of the programme was changed from *Cash Mountain* to *Who Wants to Be a Millionaire?*, lifted from the title of the Cole Porter song, famously sung by Frank Sinatra and Celeste Holm in the classic Hollywood musical *High Society*. Both David Briggs and Chris Tarrant freely admit that they thought this new title was really quite naff, but nobody could think of anything better, and what ITV wants, ITV gets ... on the whole...

There was one other more troubling hiccup though from their paymasters. ITV thought Chris Tarrant was an interesting suggestion for the host of the show, but insisted that Celador provide a list of other possible presenters for them to consider. This sent David Briggs into a bit of a panic, because he'd already pretty much promised the job to his friend Chris. The Celador team all knew Chris and they had absolute faith in his ability to wring every ounce of drama out of the game, so David quietly said to Steve and Mike that they should draw up a list of absolute TV 'drongos', and make sure that they didn't put forward any names who were potentially too good, so that Chris remained at the top of the list. (Wouldn't it be fascinating to see that document?!)

In the end common sense prevailed (which it doesn't always in television executive circles), a contract with ITV was signed, and a try-out pilot show was duly commissioned. The rest, quite literally, is television history.

This was the first television show format David Briggs had ever pitched to broadcasters, and it really was happening. I asked him how exciting that felt at the time. He readily admits, before they'd gone on air, and long before they knew just how big a hit it was going to be, that he was extraordinarily excited when ITV signed on the dotted … His baby, his creation, was going to be on television! It was thrilling!

Paul Smith, the show's Executive Producer, wanted *Millionaire* to be like no other quiz you'd ever seen. He commissioned talented young set designer Andy Walmsley to create a new type of imposing quiz show set. Andy's solution was to design a set like no other, a modern-day hi-tech take on a Roman gladiatorial colosseum.

In the end two pilot shows were made, because Paul Smith was unhappy with the look and feel of the first one. He apparently said it looked too much like *Seaside Special*, circa 1976. Andy's set worked well, but it was too brightly lit and the show was jollied along by a jaunty sing-song theme tune called 'Cloud 9', with trite lyrics, penned by bubble-gum-pop legend Pete Waterman.

Paul instinctively felt that there was something drastically wrong. That first pilot show, which was never transmitted, was way too upbeat, cheery and cosy. Despite the gladiatorial set the show still lacked tension, drama and suspense. Real jeopardy was inherently there in the potentially brutal "win a lot, or crash and burn" format, but it just wasn't coming across. Smith and Briggs both knew that beads of sweat would make much more compulsive viewing. The whole thing needed to be darker, in every sense of the word.

Paul ditched Pete Waterman's corny theme song and commissioned his old friend and musical collaborator Keith Strachan to come up with a more menacing signature tune, sans cheery vocals. Keith enlisted his talented son Matthew to help. Together they also created all those intimidating beds of tense background music and musical punctuations, which keep the contestants and viewers on the edge of their seats during gameplay. The Strachans came up with what is the quintessential quiz theme, and background music package, which is now known and instantly recognised all around the globe – and frequently emulated, but never bettered.

The other problem was the lighting. Paul called a face-to-face meeting with top lighting director Brian Pearce and told him to throw away the usual quiz show brash bright lighting rulebook, to create a dark ominous look to the show, with a threatening focus on the contestant in the middle of Andy Walmsley's life-or-death arena. It can't be overstated how much Brian and Andy changed the look of quiz shows from that day forward.

It could be argued that *Millionaire* owes as much to the darkness and portentous menace of *Mastermind* as it does to the excitement and vicarious financial avarice of *Double Your Money*.

It is no coincidence that Paul Smith insisted, once the format started to sell like hot cakes abroad, that each participating broadcaster, from whichever country, used the exact same look, and the Strachans' music. It was a guaranteed winning formula, and any departure from it would jeopardise the virtually guaranteed success of the overall *Millionaire* package, as seen on ITV.

The *Millionaire* team had created whatever the opposite is of a 'perfect storm'. A dream ticket, I suppose. The show had an addictive format, with a 'play-at-home' element, thanks to the way the questions and answers were displayed on the screen, and it had what David

Briggs calls 'shout-ability'. It had an appealing USP, by offering the biggest prize in quiz show history. It also had interesting and original play embellishments, thanks to the iconic lifelines. It looked amazing and unique, courtesy of the set design and the lighting, and the music evoked tons of drama and tension. But it had one other factor, which I believe was every bit as important – the perfect host. Chris Tarrant stole the mantle of the UK's ultimate quiz show host the very first day he fronted the show. I am certain *Millionaire* would never have become the worldwide phenomenon it undoubtedly is, without a master craftsman at the helm, showing hosts around the globe how it should be done. It simply wouldn't have happened in the same viral way if they'd given the job to Jim Bowen, Cilla Black, Phillip Schofield, Davina McCall, or even Bruce Forsyth. Chris is very sharp and was a TV producer himself, back in the day, so he intuitively knew how to steer each different game, constantly reading the contestants and their gameplay.

I've said before that being a good quiz/gameshow host is a hugely underrated job. It's probably worth quoting something I said about the job in my biography of *Generation Game* host Larry Grayson:

I know from having produced many TV gameshows over the years myself that the much-maligned role of gameshow host is a very specialised and complex skill, and much harder than it looks. The performer has to be able to multi-task on many levels for a start. He or she has to be on top of the mechanics of the game at all times, acting as judge and referee, making sure all the rules are adhered to, and that the gameplay is progressing correctly and at the right pace, whilst remembering to stay calm and in control, and ideally being funny, avuncular, informative, witty, tough but sympathetic, and charming, all at the same time. They also have to be able to ad lib their way out of any situation, so their brain has to be in gear, and their wits highly tuned, from beginning to end. It is no coincidence that all the best gameshow hosts have been highly intelligent people – Bruce Forsyth, Bob Monkhouse, Tom O'Connor and Chris Tarrant being among the cream of the British crop.

Chris also cared about the *Millionaire* contestants. He doesn't live the glamorous stereotypical celebrity lifestyle. He likes ordinary working people, and he genuinely wanted them to win, taking a real interest in them as human beings. That kind of sincerity and warmth simply cannot be faked. In addition he created many of the now world-famous *Millionaire* catchphrases, which all the other hosts use, and he pioneered the suspenseful hanging pauses before giving results, a technique which is now used (over-used in many cases!) by the hosts of every show from *Dancing on Ice* and *Strictly* to *I'm a Celebrity* and *MasterChef*. Interestingly, particularly in the early days, if you watched a foreign episode of *Millionaire*, it was like watching somebody doing an impression of Chris, just in a different language.

I asked David Briggs how much Chris's presence contributed to the global success of *Millionaire*, and, without hesitation, he said he believes that 50% of the show's success was down to Chris.

Paul Smith was confident that they had a potential hit on their hands, and he had enthusiastic support from the powers-that-be at ITV, but I think it's not unfair to say that none of them realised just what a colossal runaway success they were all unwittingly nurturing.

The then ITV Director of Programmes, David Liddiment, had such faith in the show that he made the shrewd and unprecedented decision to screen the first series of one-hour *Millionaire* episodes every evening, in primetime, for ten consecutive nights, to give it an 'event television' feel, and of course to hook viewers in. This was in September 1998. David Briggs' personal excitement reached fever-pitch, especially as he hadn't just handed the whole thing over to Celador to make – he was hands-on, working on the show, and loving every minute of seeing his baby come to life.

The unusual scheduling ploy worked, and Liddiment's faith was rewarded. Viewing figures were astronomical. By series two the show was being watched by nearly 20 million people. Broadcasters would kill for ratings like that these days.

Paul Smith says that they could tell they were on to a true winner from week one. Within the first couple of days of the very first transmissions he started to get a steady trickle of calls and faxes from foreign broadcasters, interested in buying the format. At the current time around a record-breaking 160 countries have bought the show and have created their own long-running native versions.

It was, as we have seen in this book, very common for American broadcasters, the quiz and gameshow doyens, to sell their formats to British television, but the reverse flow of programme idea sales very rarely happened. As David Briggs said to me, "You don't expect to sell coals to Newcastle, and you don't expect to sell gameshows to America." This all changed with *Millionaire*. The colossal ABC Network in America couldn't wait to get their hands on the show and had it on air by August 1999, hosted by one of their top veteran TV presenters, Regis Philbin. Once again it was a phenomenal success. So much so that the Disney Corporation also licensed the format and played it live every day as a potent tourist attraction in one of their world-famous Florida theme parks.

It is now, arguably, the most successful quiz show format in the world. David Briggs, Steve Knight, Mike Whitehill and Paul Smith became very wealthy men!

In fairness to David, I asked him when he knew that he'd created something that was going to take the world by storm, expecting him to say something about the cheques rolling in from America, but he said, "On programme two we had a young woman contestant who showed every emotion, especially when she phoned her father for help with a question and he didn't know the answer. She was nearly in tears, and he was so sorry. There was this moment of tension and real emotional attachment which almost certainly had people crying at home. That was the moment when I knew we were on to a winner."

I know David has always been a bit of a 'petrolhead', so it was no great surprise when he added that he knew he'd created a financial hit the day he went out and bought his dream car – a 007-style Aston Martin.

The press had initially been very supportive of *Millionaire*, and gave it a lot of tabloid front-page coverage. However, as is usually the case with the print media, they eventually turn. Build 'em up and knock 'em back down, seemingly being the ethos. How often have we seen that happen? After a while they started questioning whether anybody would ever win the million-pound jackpot. In America, ABC had a million-dollar winner in their first year on air, claiming the honour of giving away the show's first ever one-million top prize, anywhere in the world. It was won by a rather cocky character called John Carpenter, who smugly used his 'Phone a Friend' lifeline to call his father, not for help, but to boast that he was just about to win a million dollars! Carpenter worked for the IRS, the States' equivalent of HMRC/Inland Revenue. Him, of all people, winning a million bucks, must have gone down about as well as a bowl of two-day-old cold snail porridge! However, here in the UK, we were two years and seven series in, and there was still no sign of anybody taking away the biggest promised prize in British television history. The press started gunning for the show, saying it would never happen, then, in series eight, along came Judith Keppel.

Judith, third cousin of Camilla Parker-Bowles, now Queen Consort of the UK, was a garden designer, who lived in Fulham. She claimed to be short of money at the time, but she certainly wasn't your average quiz show contestant and appeared to be as cool as a cucumber as she effortlessly romped her way through the first nine questions to £16,000, using only one lifeline. The time-up klaxon sounded, which meant she had to complete her game in the next programme. She used her last two lifelines to get to £125,000 and then just seemed to know the answers to the remaining three boffin-grade questions. As the question setters on the programme used to say, they're only easy if you know the answer. This allowed Chris, for the first time ever, to utter the immortal words, "You've just won one million pounds!"

I know Chris well, and I know he was perhaps more emotional than Judith was. He'd been dying to say those words for two years, and he was genuinely thrilled for her. It has to be said though that Judith wasn't perhaps as cool as she appeared to be. She was very much from the 'stiff upper lip' class, but she apparently did quietly say to Chris, during a recording break, before he announced whether she had answered the final question correctly, "What will you do if I faint?" As the producers hadn't prepared a fainting contingency plan he just gave her a hug and told her she'd be fine. (Hoping he was right!) Judith looked numb and showed relatively little emotion when she was told she had won the million, but her adult daughter, who was there in the audience as her supporter, cried buckets! And at least Judith managed not to faint...

The other famous thing about that moment is that, for two years, a special effects operator called Pascal had been patiently sitting waiting for somebody to win the jackpot, so that he could press the button on his trusty confetti cannon, to shower the studio with a spectacular deluge of showbiz glitter. When his big moment finally came he pressed the button, the cannon failed, and nothing happened. The air in the production gallery turned blue with the screamed profanities emanating from the lips of the splendid director Patricia Mordecai.

Within a year the original UK version of the show had yielded two more million-pound winners. (And I think the confetti cannon worked both times!)

At the time of writing there have still only been seven people who have gone all the way to the million-pound jackpot, in this country, although one of them never got the cheque, because he was found guilty of cheating. Five of the six honest winners were during Chris Tarrant's tenure, and only one, at the time of writing this, has bagged a million from Jeremy Clarkson.

It was almost inevitable, with a million pounds at stake, that somebody would try to think of a duplicitous way of increasing their chances of nabbing it...

WHO WANTS TO BE A MILLIONAIRE? – A MAJOR SCANDAL

A lot has already been written about ex-Major Charles Ingram's fraudulent route to the programme's million-pound jackpot, but I thought it might be worth recounting some personal insights from the people in the eye of the storm.

As I'm sure you know, in 2003, after a lengthy Crown Court trial, army Major Charles Ingram, his wife Diana, and their bronchial partner-in-crime Tecwen Whittock were all found guilty of "procuring the execution of a valuable security by deception", which is legal courtroom jargon for 'cheating'. Despite the fact that Ingram answered all fifteen questions correctly, over two now infamous episodes of *Who Wants to Be a Millionaire?*, recorded in September 2001, he never did receive the million-pound prize, because of suspicions and serious concerns about the way he had arrived at those correct answers. It is now well known that he was receiving not terribly subtle coded hints, in the form of cunningly-timed loud coughs, from both Whittock, and Ingram's wife. Tecwen Whittock was another potential contestant, patiently waiting his turn in the 'Fastest Finger First' area to try for a turn in the hotseat.

The system appeared to be that, after theatrically floundering around for a while with wild guesses and preposterous theories about the correct answer, the Major would eventually read out the four answer options slowly and clearly, before committing himself to a 'final answer'. There would be relative silence in the studio after three of the four answers, but a clear cough from the direction of one of his co-conspirators, after the correct answer, would tell him which way to jump.

Perhaps one of several mistakes he made that day was the theatrical 'floundering around' and the wild guessing, because, on several occasions, he appeared to be confidently leaning towards one answer, only to have a radical change of heart, at the eleventh hour, plumping for a completely different final answer. It looked very fishy. Who does that when there's serious money at stake? (Someone who has been guided to a different answer by a coded cough, that's who!)

It is also clearly significant that the dedicated camera, which was permanently trained on Diana Ingram, seated behind her husband in the audience bleachers, catches her glancing anxiously across to her left, where Tecwen Whittock was seated, every time her husband clearly needs help.

I have heard the arguments that people cough in TV studios all the time. Now, I have spent half my life in TV studios, and, yes of course, people in audiences do cough. However, I have also sat down with Chris Tarrant and forensically viewed the unedited tapes of that show at his home, and I have never heard such obviously deliberate, unnatural-sounding and well-timed coughing as that. There is even a moment on the £500,000 question when Ingram is reasonably confident about the answer, so he bypasses their system, not reading out the four possible answers for a guiding cough, and is about to go for an incorrect final answer, when suddenly Tecwen clearly coughs, followed by an explosively coughed "NO!", which stops the Major in his tracks, making him revert to the pre-arranged system, reading out the options and waiting for a cough. And, guess what? Yep – the cough comes on the correct option, the Major does an unexpected and unexplained U-turn, changes his mind, and goes for the correct (coughed) final answer, having been so confident of a completely different answer only moments before.

There is an even more insane moment on the obscure million-pound question, which was about the mathematical name for a 'one followed by 100 zeroes' being either: googol, megatron, gigabit or nanomole. Ingram admits right away that he's not sure. If that were true, and he wasn't expecting any help, surely he'd have taken the half million, rather than risking losing £468,000 of it. However, he ploughs on, knowing full well that he has no lifelines left. (All apart from 'Cough Me the Answer' of course.)

Suddenly, reasonably confidently, he says, "I think it's a nanomole!" He waits, but there is no confirming cough, so he back-pedals and says, "But it could be a gigabit". Still no cough, so he starts suggesting he's going to give up and go. "I don't think I can do this one," he says. Undeterred though, he has one last try: "I don't think it's a megatron". No cough. He then admits, "I don't think I've heard of a googol." Suddenly there is a loud and clear cough, so Ingram says, "By a process of elimination I actually think it's googol," and then oddly admits again, "...but I don't know what a googol is..." Diana Ingram darts a look across at Tecwen, clearly worried about his help on this crucial and difficult question. There is more coughing from Whittock, as though to reassure the Major that he is certain the answer is googol. To be certain himself Ingram then reverts once more to the original system and reads each option out loud, getting a loud and clear cough once again when he says the word 'googol'. It begins to look as though Ingram is going to go for googol. Chris, totally oblivious to what is going on, reminds him several times of two critical facts – that he has never heard of the word, and there is £468,000 at stake if he's wrong! Diana looks distraught because it's beginning to look as though her husband is about to take a risk on the big one. Ingram does one last check on all four options, reading them out in turn, still getting the cough in the same place, so he announces he's going to play. Mrs Ingram looks as though she could kill him! Yet another confirmatory cough reassures him and he goes for "googol, final answer", gambling almost half a million pounds on that choice of answer – a word he'd never heard of just a few moments earlier. That is not the course of action you would expect from a responsible family and military man who clearly didn't know the answer to the question ... unless, of course, he'd had help.

Not too surprisingly it was the correct answer, and Chris told the Major he'd won one million pounds, holding up the legendary jackpot cheque, made out in his name. Ingram was in tears, his wife looked strange, as though angry, but trying to feign joy, with great difficulty.

We all know that they never got chance to cash that once-in-a-lifetime cheque, because alarm bells were

£32,000

Who had a hit UK album with 'Born To Do It', released in 2000?

- A: Coldplay
- B: Toploader
- C: A1
- D: Craig David

£125,000

'The Ambassadors', in the National Gallery is a painting by which artist?

- A: Van Eyk
- B: Holbein
- C: Michelangelo
- D: Rembrandt

£500,000

Baron Haussmann is best known for his plan of which city?

- A: Rome
- B: Paris
- C: Berlin
- D: Athens

£1,000,000

A number one followed by one hundred zeros is known by what name?

- A: Googol
- B: Megatron
- C: Gigabit
- D: Nanomole

already ringing in the production gallery.

In fact Charles Ingram's distinctly eccentric time in the *Millionaire* hotseat was spread over two programmes, with the klaxon timing him out at just £4,000 at the end of the first show, having already used up two lifelines, just to get that far. He had to come back the next day to continue his *Millionaire* journey. It has to be said that he'd really struggled to get to £4,000, so nobody on the team was expecting him to last much longer on day two. They were all expecting him to make an early exit, and were preparing to move on to a new contestant.

Interestingly there was no obvious coughing to help on day one, and it has been suggested that there was a more sophisticated, high-tech method for cheating in place at first, which involved mobile phones, although nothing has been proved. The sound department did report getting intermittent interference on the radio microphone channels during Ingram's first time in the chair, and a man, who was ostensibly a VIP audience member, was admonished several times for wandering around, brandishing a mobile phone during the recording, which was strictly against the show rules. That man, apparently, was Diana Ingram's quiz-mad brother. Make of all that what you will. Although, as a producer of many TV magic shows, I have supervised a 'mind-reading' trick where we guided a magician to accurately select the correct one of four objects by strapping phones (set to vibrate) to both his arms and legs so that we could send him a silent vibrating signal to just one of the four phones, to indicate which of the four options to choose: A being left arm, B – right arm, etc. Just saying!

The *Millionaire* team were suspicious enough to tighten up security and ban all phones from the studio the following day, but of course the Ingrams did have time that evening to come up with a low-tech alternative plan, and their private phone records showed that they had been talking at length that evening to, guess who, Tecwen Whittock.

The popular ITV dramatised (and inevitably fictionalised) version of the cheating scandal, called *Quiz*, did sort of lean towards casting doubt over their conviction, by selectively majoring on the defence's evidence in the courtroom scenes, pretty much glossing over the damning prosecution case. However, having seen and heard all the recorded evidence myself, on unedited tapes, and knowing all the relevant people, I am in absolutely no doubt whatsoever about their guilt. (Michael Sheen's portrayal of Chris was uncannily accurate, however!)

The only thing that puzzled me personally was – how did Tecwen Whittock know all the correct answers? He'd been on other TV quizzes and wasn't exactly the brain of Britain. The truth is he didn't actually know all the answers. There is one glaring example when Ingram is asked, for £32,000, who recorded the album *Born to Do It* – Coldplay, Toploader, A1 or Craig David? Pop music is clearly not one of Tecwen's strong suits, because he offers no chesty hacking help. The Major himself seems to think it's A1, not least because he has never heard of Craig David. A close-up shot of his wife at that moment shows a look of disdainful despair. She clearly knows the answer is in fact the one he's never heard of, Craig David. There is still no helpful cough from Whittock, so Ingram has to use his final lifeline – 50:50. Diana looks despairing again. The two answers left on the screen, ironically, are: A1 and, of course, the correct answer, Craig David. Mrs Ingram glances across in Tecwen's direction, presumably to see if that has helped him. Seemingly it hasn't, as he remains silent. Unfortunately, this 50:50 elimination just convinces the Major that he's been right all along, and the answer has to be A1, saying again that he has never even heard of Craig David. At this mention of the correct pop star's name there is a loud double-cough, but not from Wheezy Whittock. This time it's visibly evident that the new clever cougher is none other than Diana Ingram herself. However, her husband appears to ignore this cough from the wrong direction and announces, "I think I'll go for A1." He's still not 100% sure though, so he repeats the two remaining answers one more time. Again, when he says "Craig David" Diana can clearly be seen (and heard) coughing ostentatiously, almost choking on her third of three rapid coughs. Strangely Ingram says

It was also reported that Tecwen Whittock, more than once, was seen and heard whispering to check the answers with other 'Fastest Finger First' hopefuls, before he committed himself to a helping cough. "That's googol isn't it?", kinda thing, as fellow quizzers might well do among themselves, to prove how clever they are.

One of them though became highly suspicious of Whittock's subsequent coughing, and disapprovingly folded his arms, pointedly not applauding Ingram's startling successes.

again, "I'm going for A1", but then quickly tells Chris that's not his final answer. The director cuts to a shot of Mrs I, who is now looking decidedly peeved and frustrated. Chris is doing all the usual warnings about losing £15,000 of the money he's banked so far if he's wrong. Then, out of nowhere, the Major, using the bizarre logic that 80% of the time he's wrong anyway, decides he'll change his mind and go for Craig David – a man he's never even heard of! Diana was suddenly seen smiling for the first time in many minutes, and the production team were now on high alert.

So it seems that Tecwen Whittock didn't quite know all the answers, although he did get lucky with a lot he did know, albeit with a bit of reassurance from his neighbouring quiz buffs. No wonder Major Ingram did well. If you think about it he was actually being helped by three or four people. (Some of them unwittingly.)

In my opinion it might have been better for their chances of getting away with British TV's biggest quiz fraud if Whittock & Co hadn't known quite so much…

If Tecwen hadn't been able to convince himself that he was right about the answers to the last two tricky questions, and Ingram had quit with a very healthy £125,000, it is likely that they would have got away with their scam and walked away with the money. Any earlier suspicions of cheating would have probably been shrugged off and forgotten about. It was only by going for a highly improbable headline-grabbing million, with some seemingly inexplicable decisions, and bizarre gameplay, that serious questions started being asked behind the scenes.

It has been questioned why Chris Tarrant didn't suspect

anything at the time. I can totally understand that. He had a complex job to do, and naturally he was wrapped-up in the moment, hosting a top television programme. He readily admits that he thought Ingram's gameplay was erratic and unfathomable, and he couldn't understand how an officer, who was clearly not the sharpest sword in the regiment, was doing so well, but he had no reason to suspect him of cheating, whilst he was looking him in the eye. It wasn't as though the Major was sitting there Googling the answers on his smartphone.

I asked producer and show creator David Briggs, the man in charge that night, when he first suspected that something dodgy was going on:

"At the end of the first night I remember saying he won't be here for very long tomorrow, because he'd already used two lifelines, and he was clearly not that bright. But, once we began again on the second night, I became increasingly suspicious. By the time he'd got to a quarter of a million, I was thinking how on earth has this dingbat Major done it? And when he got to the million there were murmurings going round the whole production team, because it was obvious that something wasn't quite right, and I had to say that I agreed with them. There was definitely something fishy about his strategy. So, it was reported to Paul Smith (CEO of Celador Productions), who wasn't in the studio that night. Despite the late hour Paul drove all the way to Elstree Studios, from his home in Surrey. By now it was about 1 a.m., and he sat down with me; Ali Ratcliffe, the production assistant; and Kevin Duff, the sound supervisor, in the edit suite; and we watched the tapes over and over, until about three in the morning.

Of course, by now we had all spotted the coughing, and could see the scam for what it clearly was. Paul Smith said immediately that he was going to stop the million-pound cheque and call the police. That was the end of the Ingrams, as far as I was concerned, because they had left me with a major logistical problem, which had to be dealt with quickly..."

The problem for David was, now the police were involved, and eventually the Crown Prosecution Service, they couldn't transmit any of the recorded footage featuring Ingram, and, quite naturally, they didn't want to show somebody cheating their way to the million anyway. Worse still, the Major appeared in two separate shows. Obviously ITV couldn't afford to ditch two whole shows, and, in any case, that wouldn't have been fair on the other perfectly honest contestants who took their places in the hotseat, before and after the Major. David had to concoct a way to salvage the rest of those episodes, which meant bolting bits of both shows together, then recording more material to pad out the second show, as well as some new links from Chris to seamlessly gloss over this huge jump, in order to leapfrog invisibly over Charles Ingram's missing appearance.

People often seem to think that they watched the episodes with Ingram's win going out on ITV, but they didn't, because his sections of those two shows were never transmitted as part of the legitimate series. After the event, when the coughing scandal came to light, many clips and excerpts were shown on news programmes and in documentaries on the subject, and a lot of the footage is now available on YouTube. Scenes have even been reenacted in *Quiz*, so viewers feel as though they have seen the Major's appearance on *Millionaire*, but very few have actually seen the whole thing.

As I'm sure you can imagine, when contestants win a substantial prize on any quiz or gameshow, there is a very nice atmosphere backstage, because the winner and their supporter(s) are walking about in a state of almost disbelief, with euphoric grins on their faces, and being extremely benign and grateful to everybody behind the scenes. It's lovely to be a part of that. The Ingrams, as they came out of the studio, just having won the biggest prize in UK TV history, were extremely rude to the young female team member whose job it was to escort them, look after them and present them with a congratulatory bottle of Champagne. They then, with faces like thunder, locked themselves away in the Major's dressing-room and had a blazing row, which could be heard all the way down the corridor. That is not the normal gracious behaviour of a reasonably well-to-do couple who have just honourably and legitimately won a cheque for a million pounds.

One can only speculate what that heated argument was about, but I imagine the Major's wife was furious with him for being greedy and making a bizarre spectacle of answering the last two questions to get to the million, drawing unwanted attention and speculation as to how it could possibly have happened. She was fairly obviously the brains behind the organisation and she, like me, probably surmised that if he'd quit with a very nice £125,000, they would have almost certainly walked away scot-free with the cash, and no investigation would have ever taken place. His inept greed to go all the way, inevitably put them under the microscope. There is no doubt, when you look at the footage, that during those last few questions Mrs Ingram is looking increasingly agitated, frustrated, despairing and even angry.

There is one other thing that has always struck me about Charles, Diana and Tecwen. (Why do those names suddenly remind me of somebody saying there were three people in their marriage?) They always seemed quite shocked, almost outraged, as to how seriously their 'little scam' was taken. I'm sure they knew that they had to be discreet and covert, as any cheating would be frowned upon, and might even lead to them losing any winnings, if they were caught out. However, I feel sure that they never thought of their sneaky scheme as a criminal act, and I'm sure they never dreamed that the police would become involved, and that they would all end up with criminal records because of it. (In fact that probably wouldn't have happened if Ingram hadn't been so greedy and pushed their luck by going for the million.) It probably seemed to them like a bit of a crafty wheeze and a relatively harmless victimless scam, but fraud is fraud, and they were no Robin Hoods.

WHO WANTS TO
BE A MILLIONAIRE?
– a highly personal perspective

Disclaimer: The opinions in this chapter don't necessarily reflect the opinions of … yadda, yadda, yadda … You get my drift?

On a purely selfish level the whole *Millionaire* phenomenon was a bit frustrating for me, because I'd worked on most things that Chris Tarrant had ever done on TV and radio, in some capacity or another, from *OTT*, in 1982, onwards. I'd also (very happily) worked for Celador Productions, as a TV producer, for five years, prior to *Millionaire* coming along. In fact I remember one day Paul Smith took Chris and me out for lunch in Covent Garden and said, "What we need to find is a new show for you to produce and Chris to host". Unfortunately, *Cash Mountain* hadn't yet landed on his desk, and the entertainment shows I'd been producing for Celador were coming to a natural end, after five successful years. Paul had nothing else to offer me right away, so I reluctantly moved on and became busy as a freelance producer for a new entertainment production company called Objective Productions. This meant that I missed out on the first heady days of *Millionaire*, when it came along.

Naturally enough that initial frenzy and excitement over the show settled down, with the record-breaking viewing figures inevitably waning slightly, but it was still one of ITV's biggest series. After the show had been on air in the UK for four or five years, Chris Tarrant phoned me and asked about my availability. The first wave of *Millionaire*-mania was over, but the show was still going strong, and they were wanting to breathe some fresh air into the programme, to keep up its momentum. They were adjusting the format for the first time, which meant changing the prize ladder, dropping the first three low-scoring steps, thus ramping up the excitement by reducing the number of questions from fifteen to twelve, and they also wanted some new blood behind the scenes.

15 £1 MILLION		12 £1 MILLION	
14 £500,000		11 £500,000	
13 £250,000		10 £250,000	
12 £125,000		9 £150,000	
11 £64,000		8 £75,000	
10 £32,000		7 £50,000	
9 £16,000		6 £20,000	
8 £8,000		5 £10,000	
7 £4,000		4 £5,000	
6 £2,000		3 £2,000	
5 £1,000		2 £1,000	
4 £500		1 £500	
3 £300			
2 £200			
1 £100			

After an extremely amicable lunch meeting with genial executive producer Colman Hutchinson, I was offered a job on the show. They already had a perfectly good producer in the show's creator, David Briggs, but I could make myself useful looking after Chris, briefing him on all the contestants, and writing any script that was needed, plus any other creative assistance I could offer to the whole production team. They weren't sure what to call me, so I suggested a pretty meaningless title – Programme Associate – which I was proud to be credited as for an incredible ten years. Even at that point in the show's history it was a prestigious and exciting programme to be involved with, and to have on your CV. I already knew most of the people involved, and we had an absolute ball for seven years. It's an old cliché, but we really did become like a family. I used to genuinely look forward to each new block of studio recording days when they phoned to put them in my diary.

Now I'm sure a lot of people watch a quiz show with a jaundiced eye and think, "Greedy contestants, greedy TV companies making big profits, and callous production teams who cynically grab people off the street, exploit them and then spit them back out." Well, I can personally reassure you that this certainly isn't always the case, and it most definitely wasn't the case on *Millionaire*. We all, Chris included, became emotionally invested in the contestants, and we were genuinely thrilled and excited when a big winner came along. In truth it was sometimes even more emotional with smaller wins. We'd get some young single mother who was in debt and struggling to pay her household bills, trying her best to bring up her kids, and she might win, say, a mere £10,000. It wasn't going to put her in the headlines, like Judith Keppel, but that sort of money was completely life-changing for her, and she'd be crying real tears of absolute joy. Not only could she pay off her credit cards and the outstanding arrears on her electricity bill, but she could also take the kids on a holiday-of-a-lifetime to Disney World, or wherever. To be a part of that was genuinely heart-warming and uplifting.

I particularly remember one retired woman whose adult son had emigrated to Australia some years before and, although he'd always kept in touch with her, she hadn't seen him since. He'd married an Australian girl and had kids out there, so this woman had a daughter-in-law and grandkids she'd never met. She was a lovely woman and a doting mother, but she and her husband simply couldn't afford to fly to the other side of the planet. She started doing well on the programme, and was one of the people who had to return to complete her game in the following show. We were all absolutely rooting for her. I was an emotional wreck when she won enough for her and her husband to make that thrilling trip to Australia, to be reunited with their son, and meet their new family for the first time. We were all round the back of the set, shouting "YES!" and punching the air.

Another delightfully endearing female contestant appeared on the show. I remember her emotionally telling me that her husband was in his early sixties and had a long-term, very painful bad back, but had to keep doing hard manual labour as a builder, because he couldn't afford to retire, a fact which broke her heart. We were all in bits when she choked back the tears to announce to Chris that she couldn't wait to phone her husband because the prize money she was taking away was plenty for them to retire on, and her husband could leave work the very next day! Those moments were extremely special, and made you realise the power of a great quiz show.

The show paid off student loans, provided care for elderly family members, got hard-working people onto the property ladder, paid for weddings, honeymoons and home alterations for the parents of handicapped kids, and a huge amount was won by celebrities for many charities. Lovely.

Of course, there were contestants with less heart-tugging ambitions for their hard-earned winnings. I remember Chris asking one woman, as he often did, "If you win a few quid tonight, what will you spend it on?" She floored us all when she answered, "If I win enough, I'm going to have liposuction!" He's not often lost for words, but it left Chris with nowhere to go with that conversation. He could hardly say, "Well yes, you are a bit of a porker – you could do with it!"

Now those of you who have been paying close attention may have spotted an apparent anomaly in my personal involvement with the show. I said I worked on *Millionaire* for its last ten years, and then said that we had an absolute ball for seven years. Both those facts are true and don't in fact contradict one another.

After the show's first eight phenomenal years, Paul Smith and the creators of *Who Wants to Be a Millionaire?*, having enjoyed the embryonic bounteous period, decided to put the intellectual property rights to the format on the open market. A frantic bidding war ensued, which was won by a Dutch company called 2WayTraffic, who outbid everybody, by paying a staggering £106 million for the rights to all of Celador's shows, including of course *Millionaire* and all its many merchandising spin-offs. It was rumoured at the time that this huge sum over-stretched them as a company and led to them being taken over the following year by global media giant, Sony Pictures Entertainment. Suddenly the show belonged to Sony.

Truthfully, nothing on the ground changed much at first, and we all continued happily making the shows in the same old way. However, after a couple of years, Sony sent in a somewhat ruthless executive to shake things up. I will refrain from using the word 'hatchet-man'. He didn't particularly like what he saw when he came to observe the team in action – our cosy 'family' way of working. He told us he believed that teams were more productive when they were at each other's throats. Alarm bells started to ring!

There was an insidious trickle of insinuations that the show had always been badly produced. As I hadn't been involved right from the overnight sensational success of the first shows, I could step back objectively and see how unfair these criticisms were. It was tempting to leap to their defence and ask, "If it was so badly made how come it pulled in 20 million viewers and was such a massive hit that it attracted a record-breaking 160 countries, desperate to pay to copy the show, exactly as it was made in the UK?" But that would have no doubt been ignored, and shrugged off as sour grapes.

There were inevitable personality clashes and, in the end, Sony handed the whole show over to one of their subsidiary production companies, and a brand-new team of producers ... in the process ousting everybody else.

They made no secret of the fact that they really wanted rid of me as well, but Chris insisted that I was kept on. Unfortunately, that made me feel about as welcome as a ketchup stain on a wedding dress. They took away my production office desk, so I had to hover like a spare part, leaning against the photocopier. All the previous creative autonomy I'd enjoyed was replaced by constant scrutiny and withering disdain. No longer did I look forward to those gloriously happy studio days. Quite the opposite, in fact.

Of course, in the greater scheme of things, it's irrelevant how they treated me, but, in my personal opinion, they also irrevocably damaged the show, in their zealous quest for change (for change's sake). They'd obviously never heard the age-old adage, "If it ain't broke, don't fix it."

The big change was putting a visible clock and a strict time-limit on answering the first seven questions. Just fifteen seconds for the first two, then thirty seconds for the next five. What that did was stop Chris doing what he was best at. He could no longer tease the contestants, and prey on their uncertainties about their answers. In fact he couldn't speak at all, or he would have been accused of wasting the contestants' precious answering time. That had always been the beauty of the show – one person's individual battle against the game itself, with Chris coaxing, cajoling, prodding and questioning their decisions. That way we, as viewers, learned so much about them as human beings, making us care whether they won or lost. Every game was different. Against the clock, with Chris now effectively gagged, and questions flying like bullets, every game became pretty much the same.

It can't be a coincidence that, when *Millionaire* returned to our screens in 2018, still under the auspices of Sony, but a different subsidiary set-up, the clock had gone, and Jeremy Clarkson's producers reverted to playing the original freewheeling version.

The first Sony regime also insisted that Chris cut down on the initial chat to each new contestant, so that we could get on with playing the game. Again this stopped the audience finding out what made these people tick, and whether they were going to be a contender worth supporting or not. The knock-on effect of this inevitable loss of interest in real human players was that, latterly, the shows became predominantly charity celebrity specials. Those had always worked well, but a barrel was beginning to be scraped for guests. Bear in mind early celebrity players had included 'A-listers' like Paul McCartney, George Michael, Peter Kay, Jonathan Ross, Stephen Fry, Nigella Lawson, Simon Cowell, Joan Collins, Alex Ferguson and Terry Wogan.

By 2014, after fifteen successful years, I think Chris felt the best years were over, and he had always believed in going out while you're still on top, so he decided to leave the show, a decision which finally ended the series on ITV, at least for the time being. Personally, in many ways, I was secretly relieved.

Friends and family have often asked me what I make of the 2018 reboot, hosted by Jeremy Clarkson. I have to tell them that I genuinely can't offer an opinion as I haven't seen one. Some don't believe me, but the programme was such an important part of my life that I tell them that it would be a bit like them watching somebody else sleeping with their husband or wife. It's intensely personal. I really can't watch it. To be honest I think Chris is much more grown up and sanguine about the recent shows. It was a terrific format, so it was bound to come back sooner or later, and he'd been there and done that, which meant ITV, of course, had to find a replacement host. He was completely unfazed by the reboot.

There was a memorable day when the new executives insisted that I start introducing a new phrase of modern gameshow parlance into the script – "win big".

It's a phrase which, personally, makes me wince, and I know Chris has always hated non-grammatical colloquialisms. (He was an English teacher, for goodness' sake!)

I tried to resist, but they absolutely insisted. When we got into the studio for rehearsal, Chris took one look at the autocue and shouted over to me – "What the hell's that doing in the script, Tony? I am NOT going to say 'win big'!"

And he never did.

THE WEAKEST LINK

In August 2000 the BBC surprised viewers by launching a quiz series which offered quite a bit of hard cash by way of prizes, something they'd always baulked at in the past. Not only that, but this new quiz also started a new trend for 'nasty' game shows, where contestants were encouraged to gang up against one another, rather than the cosy "we're all in this together" teamwork we had normally associated with good ol' British fair play.

In the original Anne Robinson series nine contestants, playing as a somewhat treacherous team, and against the clock, answered quiz questions, in turn, to progress up a nine-link chain to the top target prize. A correct answer moved the team up the chain, adding money to the communal pot. An incorrect answer smashed the chain and flushed everybody's hard-earned dosh down the dunny. It was possible to safely bank the amount the previous contestant had just taken for the team, but over-cautious cowardice could be frowned upon, because that meant the next person was back at the lowest earning step of the ladder. At the end of each round the players voted off the comrade they believed was the most stupid and and/or timid, aka 'The Weakest Link'. The disgraced contestant was callously dismissed by Cruella Robinson.

The last two finalists battled it out to steal all the money won by the team, leaving the runner-up with the same as his seven 'weak' partners-in-humiliation – a big fat zero!

And, as if that wasn't bad enough, it featured a 'nasty' host, again bucking the trend for quizmasters to be kindly, encouraging and sympathetic. To be frank it didn't seem too much of a stretch for Anne Robinson to play the sadistic dominatrix, dismissing contestants with a bit less compassion than a Kray Twins' debt collector, but that seemed to suit the show.

The Weakest Link pitted nine contestants against one another in a quiz quest for cash, which involved stabbing your fellow team players in the back. (They rightly say there is no 'i' in team, but, of course, there is one in 'selfish'.)

The Weakest Link was hugely successful and, like *Millionaire* before it, attracted the attention of many overseas buyers, including that traditionally tough nut to crack – the USA. *Millionaire* had opened the door to America, but others were quick to cash in on that surprising success. Anne Robinson was even invited to fly out to the States and host the first year of *Weakest Link* on NBC.

(Interestingly Chris Tarrant had previously been offered the chance to go out to host the first American version of *Millionaire*, but he reluctantly declined, as he had other work commitments at home, and, more significantly, it would have meant a lot of time away from his family, which was a sacrifice he wasn't prepared to make, despite a huge cash incentive.)

Anne Robinson remained as the British host for eleven years, clocking up a remarkable total of almost 1,700 shows. Over the years she toned down the malevolence and was even, it is rumoured, known occasionally to smile.

After a rest of ten years, the BBC revived the show in

2021 with Romesh Ranganathan as torturer … er, sorry – host.

In fact, perhaps because all the contestants on this rebooted series were celebrities, Romesh played 'Mister Nice Guy'. He even praised players' performances. Anne 'Countess Dracula' Robinson must have been turning in her coffin, where she snoozes away her daylight hours.

The Weakest Link cash chain was similar to the prize ladder in Millionaire. They called it a chain though, to keep with the theme of 'links'. Get it?!

The big difference was that the monetary links reflected the frugality of the BBC, versus the brash extravagant cash steps ITV dare offer.

The look of the show also aped the ominous darkness of Millionaire. Here was the BBC's rival show.

Strange, though, that lovable cuddly 'Aunty Beeb' chose to go with an altogether more ruthless game.

COPYCAT SHOWS ...

With the explosion of satellite and cable channels (not to mention the massive and much-envied success of *Millionaire*) the new millennium heralded a huge proliferation of quiz and game shows.

Thanks to the ever-growing number of new channels, media advertising revenue was now being stretched and pulled in many different directions. ITV and Channel 4 no longer shared the TV advertising monopoly and took a hit, so they had to cut back on programming costs, and, let's face it, gameshows are relatively cheap to make.

Clones of already successful quiz shows started coming thick and fast – some more thick than fast. It didn't take long for ITV to jump on the 'nasty' quiz bandwagon, instigated by the undeniable success of *The Weakest Link*.

In 2001 they launched a brand new ... er, well, actually fairly derivative show, unfortunately given the schoolboy-innuendo-laden name, *Shafted*. If the Beeb had already snapped up 'Ms Mean' in the shape of Anne Robinson, then who could they find to be 'Mr Mean'? Yes, of course, Robert Kilroy-Silk. What??!! More like Mr Bean, in truth. One piece of his contrived pantomime villainy probably still has people waking up screaming at night, having nightmares about him standing on the set, doing graphic hand gestures, and, in a decidedly creepy voice, uttering the sweat-inducing words, "Their fate will be in each other's hands as they decide whether to share ... or to shaft!" AAAAAHHHH!!!!

Mr Kilroy-Silk even tried to emulate Ms Mean's way of callously dismissing failed contestants by snapping, "You're off the show!" Well, he couldn't very well say "You are the weakest link", because the weakest link was him.

I'm being slightly unkind, but then the show was more than slightly unkind, and it just wasn't the right career move for a housewife's heartthrob, who had made his name as the calm voice of middle-class, middle-England reason in sometimes heated studio debates on human issues. I suppose, up until then, he had been seen as a sort of cross between Jeremy Kyle and Santa Claus, with a dashing dash of Richard Gere thrown in for good measure. *Kilroy* was eventually cancelled in 2004, following racist remarks he had written in the *Sunday Express*. He then went on to join UKIP, before being a founding father of a short-lived breakaway anti-immigration party called Veritas, all of which pretty much brought his television career to a screeching halt. Ironic really for a man whose catchphrase, albeit briefly, had been, "You're off the show!"

The rules of *Shafted* were way too complicated to explain, and not really worth the effort, as ITV pulled it from their schedules after just four episodes had aired, with disastrously plummeting viewing figures, leaving the rest of the series gathering dust on the 'NBG' shelf, never to be seen again. Suffice to say the game was so driven by greed and back-stabbing that even the normally benign and uncomplaining Salvation Army raised a vociferous objection. Not only that, but ITV also received complaints that the name of the programme itself was offensive. Not ITV's finest hour, all in all.

There was one interesting element of the show, which was actually more like a ruthless psychological human experiment. It was a sort of end-game where the two finalists, who had battled their way to a large communal cash pot by answering quiz questions and stabbing their fellow players in the back, were given the opportunity to steal the lot, share it between them, or risk losing everything. In a secret ballot they had to decide whether to 'share or shaft'. Their choices were then revealed to one another. If they were playing nice, and both had decided to 'share', then they got half each, and a pat on the head. However, if one had decided to 'shaft' and one decided to 'share' the money, the first one bagged the lot, leaving the second (kind) one with nothing – except, presumably, a temporary loss of faith in humanity. However, that selfishness could backfire and come at a cost, because if they both decided to 'shaft' each other, then they were both sent home with absolutely zilch!

Served 'em right IMHO!

It's worth Googling "The prisoners' dilemma". That philosophical concept illustrates basically the same wickedly thorny predicament.

In 2007, ITV had another go at a 'nasty' quiz format, to rival the BBC's *Weakest Link*. This time, fortunately, it was better thought-through. This one was called *Golden Balls*, hosted by billiard-ball-headed Brummie comic, Jasper Carrott. (He's the one on top.)

Taking a leaf (stealing a leaf?) from its BBC counterpart, it included contestants playing for cash as a team, whilst secretly plotting to overthrow and deceive their opponents, in order to steal all the cash for themselves. It also had the familiarity of lottery-style balls rolling temptingly around to add a sense of chance, as well as the lure of possible fortunes to be won.

Strangely it purloined one unseemly element from the disastrously ill-fated *Shafted*. A "prisoners' dilemma" end-game. The ultimate ruthless kicker was that, at the end the show, two finalists had to surreptitiously decide whether to 'Split or Steal' the overall winnings. Just like *Shafted*, if one covertly decided to 'steal' and one decided to 'split' the money, the first one snaffled all the dosh, leaving their open-mouthed opponent, who had been perfectly happy to split the winnings, with the sum total of nothing. If they both decided to 'steal' then they were punished for their mutual greed by losing the lot. (Their loss being ITV's gain, so to speak.) But, if they both decided to 'split', then they got half the cash each ... and lived happily ever after. There must be a moral in there somewhere!

It seemed that funnyman Jasper was too nice and too comical to be a party to such chicanery, and many of his fans believed it was a waste of his prodigious talent as one of our finest stand-up comedians. It has to be said he never looked 100% comfortable in the role of quizmaster. However, the show was successful enough to go on for two years, and Jasper made around 300 episodes, and quite a few quid in the process, which he decided not to split with Billy Connolly...

Jasper Carrott was a non-executive director and major shareholder of Celador Productions. I remember reading somewhere that he made more money out of the global success of *Who Wants to Be a Millionaire* than he'd made out of a lifetime career in stand-up comedy. If that is true it's an astonishing fact!

In 2010 Channel 4 jumped on the million-pound bandwagon, offering this princely sum as a possible prize on *The Million Pound Drop Live*. It was hosted by Davina McCall, who, like a puppy at walkies-time, was predictably over-excited by the game, the set, the million-pound prize, her outfits, the contestants, the fact that they were live, and probably the absolutely B-ERRILLIANT cups of tea during rehearsals.

The twist here was that the contestants were given the million pounds right from the get-go, in real folding-ones. The problem was – keeping it! (The players should perhaps have just tasered Davina and legged it!)

Contestants either played alone, or with a partner. Davina posed a quiz question which, like *Millionaire*, had four possible answers displayed on-screen. They had sixty seconds in which to gamble their million on one of the suggested answers. If they were undecided, they could choose to hedge their bets and put some of their money on up to three possible answers. They physically put 25-grand bundles of £50 banknotes on top of trapdoors displaying the possible answers. Losing the million started as soon as they committed any cash to a wrong decision. The three trapdoors associated with the three wrong answers opened up and swallowed any money that was sitting on top of them. Providing the correct answer had some dosh on it, the contestants could keep that amount to play on the next of eight questions. It was virtually impossible to have the general knowledge and, more importantly, the absolute certainty needed to win a million pounds. I think the biggest winners they ever had, over a five-year period, were a couple who managed to cling on to just a quarter of the initial million they were originally handed.

After a three-year hiatus the show was revived as the *£100K Drop*. Obviously times were hard at Channel 4 by 2018, as the million on offer had dwindled to a mere £100,000. They say money isn't everything, but it seems, when it comes to quiz shows, sometimes it is. This new thriftier version only lasted just over a year, before it was axed.

In order to prove that the show was live there were questions about things that happened recently, even that day, plus Davina kept making pointed references to 'today', current events and that day's big news stories. Alright Davina! We believe you! We get it! It's live! Me thinketh the lady doth protest-eth too much...eth...

TEST THE NATION

The next logical step for quiz shows came with the next leap in communication technology. By the turn of the millennium, viewer interactivity was suddenly a very real possibility.

In this book I have constantly stressed the importance of the 'play-at-home' factor in any gameshow or quiz show. It's that irresistible urge to show off to anybody else in the room by shouting out the answers to the questions. We all love playing along from the safety of our favourite armchair.

Suddenly television technology allowed viewers at home to play along for real, and demonstrate how clever they really were.

The first interactive national quiz show in this country was *Test the Nation* on BBC One in 2002. It was based on a similar show which had launched the previous year in the Netherlands.

The show was very inclusive. If you weren't readily conversant with interactive TV technology, or you thought the internet was the information superhighway of the devil, technophobes were encouraged to play along using good ol' fashioned paper and pencil.

It was easier to cheat that way as well, when family members asked, "How did you do?"

The hosting honours went to a more benign and less leather-clad version of Anne Robinson, with Phillip Schofield tagging along, just because we don't see nearly enough of him on television. They also had academic experts on hand to analyse the results.

Of course it wasn't long before ITV jumped on the interactive quiz bandwagon and were offering *Great British Tests* on: driving, spelling, memory and pop, all hosted by Gabby Logan and Neil Fox.

There was a similar demographic-comparison quiz show, which aired on Sky 1 in 2007, called *Are You Smarter Than a Ten-Year-Old?*, hosted by Noel Edmonds. It pretty much did what it said on the tin.

In the *Test The Nation* studio there were celebrities, plus groups of people from various walks of life – teachers, removal men, butchers, students, fashion models, doctors, reality TV participants, scientists, van drivers, clairvoyants, and (in less woke times) blondes, brunettes and redheads.

The idea was to test everybody, both in the studio and at home, with a barrage of themed quiz questions. The aim in the studio was to see which demographic groups were the most intelligent. That allowed you at home to play along and see how you compared intellectually to all of the participating demographic groups.

Can you imagine the outcry now if you came up with a quiz format called: "Are You As Dim As a Blonde?" Different times!

BIG FAT QUIZZES

THE
BIG FAT QUIZ
OF THE YEAR

Millionaire had cornered the market for intimacy in quiz shows – just one person, every emotion exposed in a big close-up, taking on the game itself, in the hope of winning life-changing cash. *Test the Nation* had done the same sort of thing, but right at the other end of the spectrum, by allowing the whole country to take part, sitting at home, unseen. Another extreme to mine for new programme ideas was in the scope of the quiz itself. Right at the end of 2004 Channel 4 came up with *The Big Fat Quiz of the Year*, which was an epic end-of-the-year treat, with questions looking back at major events of the previous twelve months. We are used to seeing two celebrity teams going head-to-head, but, in this show, three teams of celebrities take each other on, which gives the show an even more grandiose feel, somehow.

Jimmy Carr has hosted all the *Big Fat Quizzes* so far – one each year, plus a few anniversary and decade specials thrown in for good measure. There was even an occasional series of specials which, rather self-importantly, called itself *The Big Fat Quiz of Everything*, because it asked questions on every subject under the sun.

(Isn't that just 'general knowledge', which is what nearly every TV quiz show ever made has been based on, since 1955, or am I being unnecessarily cynical?)

* * *

By the turn of the millennium there had been a massive sea change in the way new programmes arrived on our screens. Out went the bold twentieth-century TV innovators and the lone mavericks, and in came the management teams and bean-counters. Commercial success became paramount (more important it seemed than outstanding originality), so single-minded crazy risk-takers were replaced by focus groups and po-faced committees.

True creativity and innovation can only come about when there is the freedom to fail occasionally. Nobody's perfect – you just have to be right more times than you're wrong, in my view. Suddenly, in television, failure was no longer an option, so TV executives were forced to become more and more cautious about what shows they invested in. Fearing for their own survival the easy option was to commission 'safe bet' programming, rather than sticking their necks out for new and original ideas, which might possibly fail. The easiest safe bet of course is to recycle old reliable hits. It's hard to believe that *Blankety-Blank* is back on our screens yet again! What next? Reboots of *Bullseye*, *On the Buses* and *Dixon of Dock Green*?

Another easy way to create 'safe bets' is to copy the success stories of your rivals. The BBC had an unexpected hit with *Strictly Come Dancing*, so ITV jumped on the bandwagon with *Dancing on Ice*. ITV launched *Popstars*, *Pop Idol* and then *X Factor*, so the BBC countered with *Fame Academy* and *The Voice*. ITV came up with *Ant &*

Interestingly *The Voice*, having premiered on the BBC, was such an obvious ITV-style rip-off, that's precisely where it ended up.

The major channels just can't stop themselves from copying that winning formula though, because it's an almost guaranteed safe bet.

It's got to the point now where I just can't imagine the bare-faced audacity of anybody pitching their 'great new programme idea', which is a singing competition, with a panel of celebrity judges – a nasty one, a mad one, a comical one, and a ditzy one in a low-cut top who cries a lot.

... And yet they still keep coming!

Dec's Saturday Night Takeaway, so the BBC mirrored with a similarly glossy brash potpourri of entertainment snippets in *Michael McIntyre's Big Show*. (Both of which borrowed a lot from the 1990s hit Saturday night show *Noel's House Party*…)

Presumably this aversion to TV risk-taking also accounts for why nearly every new drama series is a police/murder mystery.

As we have already seen, the same sort of copycat programming was happening with quiz shows, so, when Channel 4 had success with their celebrity contestant *Big Fat Quizzes*, ITV slavishly followed with *The Big Quiz*. (No fat-shaming on the people's channel.)

In a shameless bit of self-promotion ITV made their big quiz a themed soap opera contest, with teams of cast members from their own hit soaps *Emmerdale* and *Corrie*, answering questions on their own shows.

Chris Tarrant once shrewdly pointed out to me that, in this 'safety-first' age of focus groups and committee decisions, *Monty Python* would never in a million years have made it onto our screens. He's absolutely right – and neither would other timeless classics, like *Dad's Army* or *Dr Who*. And, without *Python*, there would have been no *Fawlty Towers*, and no sublime Michael Palin travel series. Also, *Only Fools & Horses* would have been axed after series one, as a result of its initially disappointing viewer response. Some smart BBC maverick, thankfully, saw the potential and kept the faith, where bean-counters would have almost certainly chickened out and pulled the plug.

The following year they tried a similar bit of self-congratulation with a *Big Quiz* face-off between 'stars' of *Benidorm* and *The Only Way Is Essex*. A *Big Sports Quiz* was also given a whirl, but then they reverted back to the ITV flag-waving battle of their two main ITV soaps.

There have of course been other themed quiz shows over the years, specialising in pop, sport, showbiz, news, cinema, history, and television itself. They usually tend to have celebrity contestants, and I have deliberately avoided talking about most of them, as they veer towards being at the 'panel game' end of the TV spectrum, which is a different beast altogether. Classic examples being the long-running hit series *A Question of Sport* and *Have I Got News for You*.

A perennially popular themed celebrity quiz revolves around television stars navel-gazing into television itself. Noel Edmonds hosted *Telly Addicts* from 1985 to 1998, but there have been lots of others: *As Seen on TV*, *It's Only TV but I Like It*, *Show Me the Telly*, *Paul Sinha's TV Showdown*...

All of these *Big Quiz* shows have been fronted by fresh-faced Stephen Mulhern, who is rapidly becoming one of ITV's star attraction gameshow hosts.

(My personal favourite being *Catchphrase*, an addictive play-along-at-home gameshow, which Stephen has art-fully made his own.)

EGGHEADS

Quizzing was rapidly becoming such a popular pastime, both on and off television, that some of the better quizzers were becoming recognisable regulars on our screens. From personal experience I have witnessed the fact that some quizzers are so dedicated to showing off their extraordinary capacity for soaking up useless facts, trivia and general knowledge, that they crop up on multiple TV quiz shows. Contestants on *Millionaire* had often previously appeared on other quizzes, like *Fifteen to One*, *Going for Gold*, *Mastermind* and Radio 4's *Brain of Britain*. For the dedicated few of these brainboxes, quizzing becomes a way of life. Some quiz shows and TV executives didn't like the fact that these semi-professional quizzers were becoming omnipresent, but a specialist gameshow company called 12 Yard Productions spotted this inescapable reality and decided to exploit the situation, rather than rail against it. They successfully devised a new format for the BBC, featuring serial quizzers.

A supersmart selection of these career-quizzers was rounded up and they were given the name *Eggheads*. The BBC launched a new quiz show, with that title, in 2003. It pitted the wits of teams of new challengers against a resident gang of egghead quiz experts. The show was hosted by suave news presenter and journalist, Dermot Murnaghan.

Some of the serious quizzers had become celebrities themselves. In fact it could be argued that, by the time this show launched, regular egghead Judith Keppel,

Millionaire's first millionaire, was more well-known to the general public than Dermot.

In 2008 Jeremy Vine entered the frame and hosted some of the shows, whilst Dermot was off recording *Eggheads* spin-offs. By 2014 Jezza had taken over altogether. Thanks to the dreaded fun-sponge Covid the BBC 'rested' the series in 2020. It seems they pretty much forgot about it, much to the chagrin of Jeremy Vine, who welcomed the move to Channel 5 in 2021.

THE CHASE

By now the two main terrestrial broadcasters were very much going tit for tat on programming, so it was almost inevitable that ITV would want a new show featuring quiz experts, inspired by the success of *Eggheads*. As usual though they had more money to throw at such a project.

To me, *The Chase* seemed like an unlikely hit, but the creators and the producers have proved me totally wrong. (In my defence, I'd ask you to thumb back a few pages and remind yourself of ITV's initial reaction to *Who Wants to Be a Millionaire?*)

In fairness, twenty-five years ago, I was pushing the name Bradley Walsh as a new rising television star, but ITV didn't want to know. I said, "Mark my words. One day he'll be bigger than Michael Barrymore!" Barrymore was the top-earning TV star of the 1990s. Funny how times change!

Is there nothing former footballer Bradley can't do on TV? If you spot him reading *News at Ten* and doing a bit of baking on Channel 4, he's officially done the lot! I knew he would.

The Chase is a show that proves none of us so-called professionals know anything really. We just have to be better at guessing than most people. If you'd told me back then about a show where a bunch of super-smart clever-dicks try to stop nice ordinary people from winning money, I would have said it had no chance. (But then if you'd told me in 2005 that a show about opening cardboard boxes to show how much money was printed inside the lid was going to be a massive hit, I would have called the men in white coats.) We none of us know anything.

To stop myself appearing too stupid I'd like to quote something top Oscar-winning Hollywood screenwriter William Goldman famously said in 1983 about never losing faith in what you believe is a good idea:

"Nobody knows anything. Not one person in the entire motion picture field knows for a certainty what's going to work. Every time out it's a guess and, if you're lucky, an educated one."

It's true, of course. If Hollywood moguls really were as smart as they claim to be, there would never be any box-office disasters or cinematic 'turkeys' ... and we all know that there are plenty of those.

Nevertheless, as I write this, I still can't believe what I am about to say, as I sum up the ethos of *The Chase*. Four ordinary decent people answer general knowledge questions to amass as much prize money as possible. Nothing untoward so far – perfectly standard quiz show fayre. BUT! Then a 'chaser', a professional quizzer and renowned general knowledge luminary, paid by ITV, attempts to steal that money back off the players.

OUCH!

Is it just me, or does that sound a bit like Robin Hood going over to the dark side? Robbing from the poor to give to the rich...

Of course, it's compulsive viewing, and that dark jeopardy works really well, despite the fact that it appears to fly in the face of all decency in quiz shows. Most programmes want their contestants to win! In fairness, naturally, quizmaster Bradley is on the players' side and

is their celebrity friend and cheerleader. The set is cleverly designed so that the 'nasty' chasers are kept aloof and way more than arm's length away. I suppose that stops any fisticuffs.

My first thought, as a reasonably upright citizen, is why don't the chasers throw a couple of questions and pretend they don't know the answers, in order to let the contestants keep their money? If only life were that simple! For a start the production team would be quick to replace the chaser if there was ever any suspicion that was happening. More importantly though those chasers really do want to win and answer those questions correctly. Their quizzing pride is at stake. It's not that they are heartless or unkind, but, in that moment of Bradley firing questions at them, they aren't thinking, "Perhaps those people need the money," they are simply thinking, "I know a lot of stuff, and I am going to amaze people by answering correctly as often as humanly possible. I want to get these right!"

By 2019 ITV had realised just what a winner they had on their hands, and launched the spin-off show, *Beat the Chasers*, where members of the public could take on up to five of the Chasers to play for serious cash sums.

In 2008 I produced a series of gameshows called *It's Not What You Know*, starring Chris Tarrant. Contestants had to predict whether celebrities answered quiz questions on specialist subjects rightly or wrongly. I needed the quiz questions writing and verifying, so I brought in a very bright but shy young northern quizzer called Jenny Ryan. She sat quietly in the office working super-efficiently for weeks, hardly speaking to anyone, no makeup, wild hair, and wearing clothes that begged not to be noticed. You can imagine my surprise when, in 2015, she first appeared on *The Chase* as the vivacious Vixen. I didn't see that one coming!

Working under pressure Jenny had needed assistance, so she asked if she could bring in her quiz-champion friend, Olav Bjortomt, who was even more painfully shy and quiet. He is now one of Channel 5's *Eggheads*.

I didn't see that one coming either!

ONLY CONNECT

This rise of the quizzers was almost inevitably going to lead to the ultimate quizzer's quiz. Back in 2008 minority cerebral channel BBC Four came up with the perfect solution – *Only Connect*. As it's still running fourteen years later, and has been promoted to the more accessible viewer-friendly BBC Two, it must have a dedicated cult following, despite the fact that it flies in the face of everything I've said about the importance of being able to play along at home. Having said that, the geeky fans of such a geeky show, are probably more than capable of playing along at home. Maybe it's just me who is too baffled and bewildered to shout out all the answers at the television!

There have, of course, been other successful precedents which break the golden rule. I can't imagine that too many ordinary viewers from Birmingham, Slough, Glasgow and Hull, watching *University Challenge*, are quicker off the mark on the Chekhov and opera questions than the bespectacled nerdy prodigy from King's College Cambridge.

On *Only Connect* the often esoteric questions are deliberately and consciously convoluted and tortuous in their construction. They are all to do with tenuous or obscure connections and sequences. Somewhat inevitably the contestants are teams of rather intense individuals. It's almost surprising to find they have enough friends to form a team of three. I saw an observation somewhere that they all look as though they cut their own

hair. I couldn't possibly comment!

I've very carefully avoided calling them nerds and geeks, although the show's host, the splendid Victoria Coren Mitchell, isn't nearly so coy. She can be positively cutting. It's an inspired bit of casting as her sarcastic wit cuts through a lot of the dry dullness of the competitors, and her femininity is a much-needed counter-balance to the predominantly male, celibate-looking clique who take part.

Victoria is also fiercely intelligent, so you can believe that she is even smarter than they are, and her sharp sense of humour is a breath of fresh air in what could have been a deathly experience.

RICHARD OSMAN'S HOUSE OF GAMES

Like *Only Connect*, *Richard Osman's House of Games* has convoluted questions, which require lateral thinking and the ability to come up with answers that go against all logic, so it is aimed at a slightly more cerebral audience. It is more accessible though and a lot less geeky, so you do stand a chance of playing along at home, if you really concentrate hard.

The show's do-ability means it can be played by our brighter celebrities, which makes it lighter-hearted, and gives it a nice cosy teatime feel, especially as they are all sitting in comfy chairs, playing for calculatingly naff prizes. Of course they all want to win, and certainly don't want to look foolish, but there is little or no killer instinct creeping in. For the viewer it's more about playing along at home and trying to beat the celebrities than caring about which one of them wins.

The programme is a mish-mash of all sorts of disparate games and quiz elements, some of which work better than others, and some are more addictive than others, but there are enough interesting rounds to hold the attention of somebody who wants to give their grey cells a bit of a workout. It's fair to say that none of the games contain easy or straightforward quiz questions, so it's definitely not a show to casually watch, or have on in the background over a mealtime chat.

Richard Osman is extremely quick-witted – I love to

see him on comedy panel games, like *Would I Lie to You* and *Have I Got News for You*, where he can genuinely hold his own against the spontaneous razor-sharp wit of Lee Mack and Paul Merton. His easy laid-back style suits his *House of Games*, and, because he's so bright himself, you feel as though you are in safe hands with him as host.

Some of the current gameshows are trickier to define as a straightforward quiz, and therefore it becomes harder to decide whether they fall within the remit of this book. I have decided to include *House of Games*, because, even though it is played by celebrities, it definitely isn't a panel game. It also sits nicely alongside *Only Connect* as a quiz which is aimed at a non-passive thinking audience.

I remember once, in a rare quiet moment during my time working as a producer at Celador Productions, Paul Smith, the CEO, asked me to spend a morning looking through his bottom drawer of gameshow and quiz ideas which had been sent in to him over the years. These were all bits of formats which had some appeal or merit, but either weren't fully thought-through or didn't sustain for long enough to make a whole programme. He wanted me to see if there were any interesting game snippets which could be merged together and turned into a whole show. *Richard Osman's House of Games* appears to be exactly that.

POINTLESS

I asked David Briggs, the creator of *Who Wants to Be a Millionaire?*, what he considers to be the best quiz show since *Millionaire*. After a moment's thought, and a brief caveat that he probably hadn't seen absolutely every new quiz format, he said he believed that *Pointless* was the best and most novel recent show. His reasoning was that it has a unique and interesting way of framing the questions.

It seemed like every variation had been tried with quiz shows – bigger and bigger cash prizes, single contestants, vast numbers of contestants, cross-fertilisation with other games, like snooker, darts and noughts & crosses, or new quiz format advances had been driven by emerging technology. Fundamentally though, they all still relied on the simple staple of asking a general knowledge question and hoping for the correct answer. Suddenly *Pointless* questions were coming at you with a whole new perspective and from a very different direction.

For obvious reasons a quiz show host or adjudicator's nightmare is a question which has multiple correct answers. For example: "Name a British county with a coastline". It's a long list. There are LOTS of them! Which counties do you accept or reject? If someone answered "Wiltshire", would you know instantly whether they were correct?

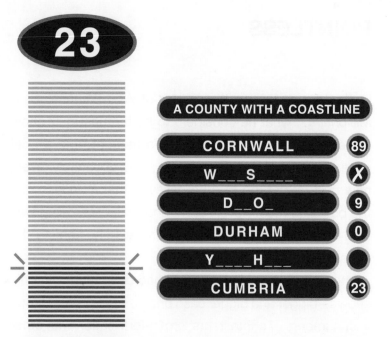

23

A COUNTY WITH A COASTLINE

CORNWALL	89
W___S____	X
D__O_	9
DURHAM	0
Y____H___	
CUMBRIA	23

Uniquely the questions on *Pointless* are deliberately designed to have multiple correct answers, and have been tested on a panel of 100 random people. The show contestants have to try to speculate which are the most obscure of those correct answers – the ones which the 100 test pilots DIDN'T think of. Over ninety of them will probably have remembered that Cornwall has an obvious coastline, so it's not a good answer to go for in the studio, as it would score over 90 points. So maybe try Durham, or Cheshire? If none of the 100 question-testing panel guessed Durham, then that is the Holy Grail – a 'pointless answer', which scores a much-coveted zero on the scoreboard.

Yes – the other novel twist is that the winners are hoping to score as few points as possible! Nice!

The show is undeniably a phenomenon. At the time of writing, over 1,500 episodes have been made, since 2009, plus 250 celebrity specials.

The original hosts were Alexander Armstrong and the show's creator, Richard Osman. Again, at the time of writing this, Alexander is still going strong, but Richard has retired to do other things and guest co-presenters are being tried out.

And there is yet another layer of jeopardy, because your answer has to be correct. So, if you did guess "Wiltshire" as a county with a coastline, then you'd be wrong and would be penalised with a maximum score of 100 unwelcome points.

The show has several appealing features.
For a start there is the opportunity for the co-host to reveal deliciously trivial details about the answers, something Richard Osman always revelled in.

And, for some strange reason, there is something highly satisfying and exciting about watching the graphic display whizzing down the number of survey panellists who went for a particular answer, just hoping for it to stop on a low number, or possibly a 'pointless answer'...

AND – bearing in mind our brutally savage TV critics – one can't help admiring the courage and self-belief, bordering on reckless professional suicide, of calling your brand new show "Pointless"...

TENABLE

In true TV copycat tradition it wasn't too long before ITV came up with a similarly different way of presenting the questions in a quiz.

Tenable again uses questions with multiple answers – ten, to be precise, which fill ten blank lines on a rising electronically-lit pyramid. Quite a bit like the descending graphic display on *Pointless* there is a moment of tension as the nail-biting music emphasises the graphics ascending the pyramid to determine whether an answer is 'tenable' or not.

Like *Pointless* it's a smart idea with a strong playability factor for the viewers at home. Initially I thought they had made a rod for their own backs in that there is a finite limit to lists of exactly ten things, but they have overcome that by posing questions like: Name the FIRST ten James Bond films. It's a much harder question than "name any James Bond film", but it gets round the intrinsic flaw.

In *Tenable* the five contestants, playing as a team, see the question, then the team captain nominates one of them to play that particular round. That person has to guess as many as they can of the ten possible answers. The more they guess the more money they win – although they have to get at least five of the possible answers before they win a quid ... well, a thousand quid, to be fair. An incorrect or 'untenable' answer is allowed only once. A second one means that contestant is eliminated from the game and they lose any money they've won. Harsh!

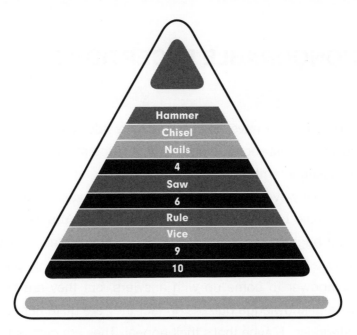

Top ten things found in a joiner's workshop

They have also tried displaying a list of ten clues which have to be turned into ten answers, but that somehow doesn't seem as satisfying to play.

On *Pointless* the contestants win by guessing the most obscure of the list of possible answers to a broad question … on *Tenable* they win by knowing ALL the possible answers.

Warwick Davis makes an engaging, genial, amusing and competent quizmaster, having already cut his gameshow host teeth on *Celebrity Squares*.

He was replaced for a series in 2021 by Sally Lindsay, due to his previous commitments on major acting projects.

HONOURABLE EXCEPTIONS

Now, I know I have been trying to restrict this book to definable quiz shows, without straying too much towards gameshow territory, which, I confess, has at times been tricky. However, I did also point out that it was my book, so I could break my own rules occasionally. You see it's been bugging me that I haven't been able to talk about two classic TV game formats, which require thought and brainpower to come up with answers, but they are not general knowledge quizzes. In fact they are quite hard to categorise. Maybe that's their appeal. They are different.

I'm talking about my personal favourite TV games *Catchphrase* and *Family Fortunes*.

What do they have in common? The one thing I have banged on about throughout this whole book – the play-at-home factor. Both shows have it in spades. I defy anybody to watch either of them, without feeling the need to shout out suggestions or possible solutions to the onscreen riddles. None of them require any great intellect, or that quizzers' in-depth accumulation of knowledge – just a bit of experience of everyday life, a familiarity with popular culture, and an everyman's use of colloquial English. They can be played by just about anybody, from any walk of life.

Catchphrase is a cracker of a game, which was created in, where else but the USA. Strangely though it only ever ran for a few months in the States, way back in 1985. It was not a success and was never re-commissioned. Clearly ITV got something right, which their American counterparts failed to do, because it instantly became a big hit here and ran consistently from 1986 to 2002. The revival, which hit the air in 2012, is still enjoying prime-time glory to this day.

> The game couldn't be simpler. As the host says, "Just say what you see!" Graphically animated scenes play on a huge screen, giving evolving clues to a well-known 'catchphrase'. Contestants buzz in to be first to identify that phrase. Basically that's it.
>
> I've said before the very best gameshows are always simple.

The original version was hosted by low-key Irish comedian Roy Walker, another gameshow export from the club comic series *The Comedians*. He ran the show for its first thirteen years. I'd almost forgotten, but there were then briefly two other hosts: Nick Weir, from 2000 to 2001, then Mark Curry, who fronted a daytime version in 2002, which didn't really work (through no fault of Mark's) so the show was quietly rested.

My favourite host, and I'm happy to admit I am totally biased, is the current incumbent, Stephen Mulhern, who has made the show his own since its welcome revival in 2012.

I worked with Stephen a lot in the early 2000s, helping him grow from a slightly raw (but clearly talented) teenage Butlins Redcoat/CITV linkman, to the fully-fledged presenter you see today, who is now one of ITV's biggest names. He was a quick learner, a charismatic performer,

100% professional and he is also a thoroughly nice human being. That is an all-too-often rare combination. Told you I was biased!

What the current version benefits from, as well as its host, is the huge 21st-century advance in computer graphic technology. The animations are so much better than the old, somewhat clunky ones from the early days. The current ones are modern works of television art.

I'm sure everybody does it, but I sit at home, glued, desperately trying to beat the contestants or the celebrities to the identification of the phrase in question. It is hugely addictive, and fun to play against whoever else is in the room with you.

I suppose I should mention the show's resident animated character, Mr Chips, but then again, why should I? He never mentions me...

It has to be said that the producers' definition of a 'catchphrase' is somewhat flexible. I think they have always used song, movie and TV show titles, but quite often they use single words, like 'butterfly'. I totally understand why, but it's a little harsh to then hear contestants being amusingly rebuked for a wrong guess of a real phrase with, "That's not a catchphrase, it's just a word!"

(It's also a sign of my age that I don't always recognise modern colloquial sayings. I turn in despair to my wife, shrug, and say, "Since when was that ever a catchphrase? Never heard of it!" Yes – say what you see – 'sore loser'...)

Family Fortunes was once mentioned to me, by somebody who knew TV and radio well, as the cleverest format ever invented. I see what he means. It's a game about real people. In a way it was a TV 'people show' before the phrase had even been coined. Like *Pointless* these days, there is some preparation work before the game can happen. One hundred ordinary members of the public are 'surveyed', as the show calls it. Basically they are asked some very simple rudimentary questions:

Name something blue
Name an item you'd take with you to the beach
Name a grumpy character from a sitcom
...etc, etc...

Of course, again like *Pointless*, there is no one correct answer, there are multiple correct answers. In fact on *Family Fortunes* the answers don't even have to be correct. If enough of the 100 surveyed people said it, then it becomes a correct answer, by default.

Their answers are kept secret and pre-stacked in the show computer (named 'Mr Babbage' in the early days of the show), in order of how many of the 100 people said each answer.

Taking the example of 'something blue' – the top-scoring answer would probably be 'sky', then maybe 'sea', etc. They usually seem to go for 5 or 6 of the highest scoring answers, which are hidden from view at first. Contestants in the studio are then asked the same question. If they say 'sky', then that lights up on the board, and is revealed as the top scoring answer. Good news for the contestant, because their job is to identify all of the answers from the 100 people surveyed, especially the top-scoring one. If the contestant had said "police uniform", and none of the surveyed 100 had come to the same conclusion, then that answer is declared wrong and is greeted by the iconic "Uh-Urrrr!" buzzer.

The contestants play as families, so other family members can attempt, in turn, to identify the other survey answers hidden on the computer board. But they are only allowed three "Uh-Urrrrs!", then it's game over for that family, and their rivals can attempt to steal their winnings by guessing correctly. If they fail to steal, then the original family keep their hard-earned dosh.

It maybe sounds complicated written down, but it really isn't.

You see what I mean about it being a 'people show' though? You have real people in the studio trying to guess what other real people said to the same question. It's not about knowing intellectual facts or nerdy trivia, it's actually all about second-guessing your fellow man, or woman.

Of course that has led to some hilarious moments over the years…

- A woman when asked that question, "Name something blue", actually said, "My cardigan!" As though the 100 surveyed people, who had never met her, would have given that answer! Host Bob Monkhouse, ever the professional, kept a straight face and said, "Let's see if it's up there…" "Uh-Urrrr!"

- Name a yellow fruit – "An orange"

- A non-living object with legs – "A plant"

- Name one of Harry Enfield's characters – "Sooty"

- A famous Royal – "Mail"

- Something that flies without an engine – "A bicycle with wings"

- Something a blind person might use – "A sword"

- Something that makes you scream – "A squirrel"

- Name a way of toasting someone – "Over a fire"

That last one got a huge laugh from the audience and host Les Dennis used his catchphrase, "If that's up there, I'll give you the money meself!" expecting to hear the "Uh-Urrrr!" buzzer. To his shock and embarrassment it WAS up there on the board – 12 of the surveyed 100 had said the exact same thing. You see what I mean about a 'wrong' answer can become right, by default.

It's a really fun game to play at home with your own family, because you can't help wanting to guess what the survey answers were.

The game was again based on an American format, which they called *Family Feud*. It started over here in 1980, in the very safe hands of Bob Monkhouse, who immediately established it as a funny must-see hit show. In 1983 though Max Bygraves took it over, presumably thinking it looked easy. If one variety entertainer can do it – anybody can. He managed to prove to himself, and to the public, what I have said all along, that being a successful gameshow host is MUCH harder than it looks. Max blundered his way haplessly through the first shows, and never really seemed to fully get the hang of it before his contract, mercifully for everybody, ran out. The show was rested for a while, but it was brought back in 1987, with amiable Les Dennis in charge. I think he surprised everyone with how well he coped, and it became his domain for the next fifteen years.

Strangely a cheap daytime version was then attempted, with a little-known host, which killed the show off for a long period. Vernon Kay successfully brought it back yet again in 2006, and it's still around now, with Gino D'Acampo as the host – making it one of the longest-running and most-watched gameshows on British TV.

Personally I'm not sure about genial Gino as the host. Firstly his not inconsiderable ego doesn't appear to be too keen on sharing the limelight with ordinary people, but I'm not sure it would work with any foreigner at the helm. Believe me, I'm not being racist, but I think you have to understand the quirky way British people think and speak to make sense of the game, and the sometimes oddball answers they give, allowing the host to mine the inherent comedy. Gino too often just looks baffled. I'd love to see somebody bright like Victoria Coren-Mitchell, Lenny Henry or Ross Noble give it a go, but I'm sure it's not their kinda thing.

AT THE TIME OF WRITING THIS ...

Well, that just about brings us up to the present day, and some of the really great quizzes, the perennial classics, are still on our screens:

University Challenge – over sixty years on from its first transmission

Mastermind – over fifty years on from its first transmission

Who Wants to Be a Millionaire? – twenty-five years on from its first transmission

Perhaps it's no coincidence that all three of these shows use some of the toughest general knowledge questions of all, and really stretch their contestants' brains to the max. Only one has a significant prize in monetary terms, so, interestingly, that isn't necessarily a 'must' for long-running success.

It seems that quiz shows are more popular than ever. There are a large number of recently created ones, and still they keep coming, with all sorts of new novel twists and gameplay USPs:

ITV have Stephen Mulhern's *Rolling in It* and Ben Shepherd's *Tipping Point*, both of which combine quiz questions with the playing of oversized amusement arcade machines.

The BBC have aired big-money quizzes with Michael McIntyre's *The Wheel* and Danny Dyer's *The Wall*.

(I'm guessing, after having had success with both *The*

Wheel and *The Wall*, the BBC probably have their finest think-tank beavering away on *The Whale*.)

Channel 4's favourite edgy gameshow host Jimmy Carr is now fronting a more traditional quiz show for the channel – *I Literally Just Told You*. Richard Bacon devised the format, which cleverly subverts the genre by asking questions where the answers have already blatantly been right there in plain sight, during the show at some point. It relies on the undeniable truth that most people's short-term memories are pretty poor, so you kick yourself for failing to remember what you saw or heard just minutes before. There's a very clear play-at-home element, but perhaps not a terribly reassuring one.

ITV have also tried out various new permutations of quiz formats in recent years:

Gameshow host favourites have endorsed new quizzes. Bradley Walsh has fronted *Cash Trapped* and *!mpossible*, and the omnipresent Phillip Schofield turned quizmaster on *5 Gold Rings*.

New ITV celebrity quizmasters have also thrown their hats into the ring – former footballers Gary Lineker and Ian Wright, with *Sitting on a Fortune* and *Moneyball* ...

What is notable is that Aunty Beeb seems to have totally lost her squeamishness about giving away large amounts of cash. Both *The Wheel* and *The Wall* offer life-changing amounts of prize money, courtesy of the licence payers.

Could this be a mistake at a time when the BBC and its compulsory licence fee is coming under political scrutiny?

comedian Lee Mack, with *The 1% Club*. Even potty-mouthed chef Gordon Ramsay has had a go, with *Bank Balance*, swelling his own in the process. And, somehow, he managed it without calling anybody a "******** stupid ****".

Again I freely admit that I have not, by any means, included every single quiz show, but hopefully I have covered all the ones which have been significant to the evolution of the genre. I do apologise if I've missed a personal favourite of yours.

One long-running ITV series I know I've missed was called *Gambit*. It was another 'pontoon'-based quiz, not unlike the US's ill-fated *Twenty-One*. The aim of *Gambit* was to correctly answer questions, in exchange for pontoon playing cards, trying to reach a perfect '21'. I don't have too much more to say about it though, even though it ran for twenty years, from 1975 to 1995, and had three different quizmasters over that time: Fred Dinenage, Gary Thompson, and one of my personal favourite gameshow hosts, Tom O'Connor.

Gambit was one of those tricky hybrids between quiz and gameshow, which have been a bit of a grey area for me and my remit here. I'm sure you can think of many others I've omitted.

When I started writing this book it was suggested that I should cover all gameshows and panel games, as well as quizzes. Thank goodness I didn't listen. You wouldn't have been able to lift it! (And I'd still be on *Cheggers Plays Pop* ... dreading what I was soon going to be writing about *Pets Win Prizes*.)

So what next for TV quiz shows? If I knew, I'd be

retiring on a very big yacht in Monte Carlo, but you can be sure that somebody will come up with yet another new exciting twist, and future generations will still be watching question-and-answer quizzes long after we're all playing 'Fastest Finger First' for a chance to get through the Pearly Gates, or be eliminated and fast-tracked to Hell, with St Peter asking, "But have you enjoyed your day?"

If you think you might be the one to create the next big idea for quiz shows, my advice is 'keep it simple'. Usually the best formats are exactly that. One of the hardest jobs in a quiz series is succinctly, but clearly, writing the host's opening explanation of the show and its rules in episode one. If that introduction is long-winded and complicated then the chances are that the show is also too complicated, and may end up never getting beyond the pilot stage.

* * *

Just before I finish I'd like to pay tribute to the great unsung heroes of the quiz world – the backroom question-setters. We never even give them a thought, but they have been the life-blood of every quiz show ever aired. I know from personal experience that it isn't easy to write good quiz questions. It sounds obvious, but they have to be indisputably right, for a start. In fact there is a whole other quiz show role for people called 'question verifiers', whose sole job it is to forensically check and, if necessary, correct every single question, in the hope of avoiding messy disputes.

Mistakes do sometimes still happen, and it's not pretty when they do. When Laurence Llewelyn-Bowen and his wife were on a celebrity special of *Millionaire* they did really well and got as far as the million-pound question, which was about the motto of the United States. Their answer was deemed to be wrong, so they were devastated to lose £468,000 of their half-million winnings for their favourite charity, a children's hospice. The validity of the question was queried immediately after the event, and, embarrassingly, the question was found to be ambiguous, and therefore their answer wasn't necessarily wrong after all! Awkward!

The Llewelyn-Bowens had to be invited back the following week to play another (different) million-pound question. They didn't know the answer, but they were able to quit with their heads held high, and their hard-earned half million restored, making them the show's biggest celebrity charity winners, to date. At least the story had a happy ending, but it must have caused a few sleepless nights for the poor question setters and verifiers.

Quiz questions have to be pitched correctly for each show – not too hard and not too easy. Even on tough quizzes the questions can't be totally unfathomable. Nor does the producer want everybody going home with a million pounds, just for knowing that the capital of France is Paris. Very often the difficulty has to be pitched on a sliding scale, so that the questions start fairly easy and accessible, then get harder as the jeopardy (and prize) gets greater.

They also have to be straightforward and the right sort of length. Long complex questions are boring and sometimes they have to fit legibly into a graphic box, which only allows a certain number of characters.

Questions must be unambiguous – if it's a question about *Star Trek* or *Mission Impossible*, do you mean the original TV series, or the more recent Hollywood movie blockbusters? If it's a mythology question about, say, the Goddess of Love, it's important to differentiate between Greek and Roman mythology, because the Greek goddess of love was Aphrodite, and her Roman counterpart was Venus.

Answers must also be verifiably accurate. It's dangerous to ask questions about the longest, tallest, heaviest, smallest, etc, because somebody will dispute it. There is still an argument raging about the longest river in the world – some say the Nile and some say the Amazon. I think a lot depends on what you define as the source of the two rivers, but you don't want that lively geographical debate going on during a quickfire, fingers-on-buzzers round, where there is serious money at stake. Somebody's going to get hurt!

First and foremost though, questions should be interesting. I don't know about you, but I'm not a fan of quiz questions about dates … "In what year was Custer's Last Stand? 1863, 1876, 1885 or 1892?"

As Rhett Butler famously said, "Frankly, my dear, I don't give a damn!" When I hear the question I don't care and can't be bothered to guess, and I still don't care when I hear the correct answer. (1876 apparently … Yawn!)

Ideally the answer should be interesting, especially if you didn't know it.

Chris Tarrant and I use a question in our live charity quiz which we both love, because it's a fascinating revelation and a wonderful bit of pub-bore trivia:

The Beatles had the top two best-selling singles of the entire Swinging Sixties, but which artist or group recorded the third best-seller of that pop-dominated decade?

A. Procul Harum
B. Ken Dodd
C. Engelbert Humperdinck
or D. Tom Jones

The answer is – Ken Dodd! Who knew??!

I think that's a rather neat and nifty end to a book about quiz shows, so...

"A very goodnight from all of us here, and see you next time!"

How **GOOD** a **Quizzer** are **YOU** ?

Jeremy Beadle used to host a huge annual pop quiz in a massive venue in London, which raised a lot of money for his favourite charity, Children with Leukaemia. It was a serious competitive quiz, but there was also a good meal, lots of dancing, singing, comedy, heaps of insanity, and I have to say the odd 'sweet sherry' was consumed as well. As Jeremy sadly became more and more ill, towards the end of his short life, Chris Tarrant volunteered to stand in for him on a couple of occasions, as it was such a long, crazy and exhausting night, lasting nearly five hours. I went along to support Chris in this sad, but bitter-sweet duty.

A year or so after Beadle's sad passing Chris was made President of The Lord's Taverners, the UK's leading youth cricket and disability sports charity, of which he'd been a proud and active member for many years. They do incredible work, raising huge amounts of much-needed cash for disabled and disadvantaged kids from all over Britain. It was a great honour for Chris, especially as previous presidents had included many of his personal heroes, the likes of Eric Morecambe, Sir Terry Wogan, Ronnie Corbett and Sir David Frost, to name but a few cricket-mad charitable benefactors. Chris phoned me and said, as their new president, he was going to do a UK tour of the many Taverners' regional branches, and he wanted to make each visit a fundraising, but fun, event. He said, "What I'd really love to do is something like Beadle's marathon pop quiz." He was still very much at the helm of *Millionaire* at the time, so it seemed like a great idea.

In most rounds each question is introduced by an extract from a pop song. As the evening unfolds, and more 'fine wine' gets consumed, the increasingly enthusiastic audience start dancing and singing along, so the musical extracts get longer and longer. Chris is a past master at getting a crowd going, so it has to be seen to be believed. After nearly five hours we end on things like 'New York, New York' and 'You'll Never Walk Alone', which nearly lift the roof off the function room.

Even though Chris's Taverners presidency only lasted two years, we keep getting invited back to do more and more. We must have been doing them now, several times a year, Covid permitting, for around fifteen years. Each one seems to raise around £20,000 to £30,000, sometimes more, so we must have raised nearly a million pounds by now. It has become a victim of its own success and we have been asked to stage the same event for other worthy causes – usually for handicapped children with special needs. It's very gratifying to be a part of it all.

I write all the quiz questions, and I keep refreshing them and replacing them from time to time, which means I have accumulated quite an archive. I thought I would put some of them as an appendix to this book, so that readers can test themselves. My supportive publisher and friend, the brilliant David Burrill, thought I should explain where these questions have come from, and why they exist, hence this preamble.

Our target audience are reasonably well-to-do people of a certain age, who are more than ready to let their hair down, but are also willing to dig deep for the charities. I think it's what's called a win-win situation. Everybody has a great night and the charity pockets a lot of dosh. Because of this target demographic you will see that the quiz is aimed at, shall we say, a 'mature' audience, who still know how to party! So, a lot of the popular culture questions tend to be nostalgia-based. However, I hope even those are on such iconic subjects that everybody stands a chance. In Round 2 you will find that the multiple-choice questions are more general knowledge-based.

I should perhaps add that, whilst I am always pretty meticulous with my fact-checking, I didn't have the TV quiz show luxury of a paid team of question verifiers to cross-check me. I have only once had a quiz night question challenged (it was about Gary Barlow, and it isn't in this book!). I'm still not sure who was right, but the young, inebriated London woman was positively abusive with me, shouting and ranting, as though I had ruined her life. In the end I had to point out that I don't get paid for doing this, I do it out of the goodness of my heart for a very good cause.

I sincerely hope you won't find any unintentional errors, but, if you do, please be a little more forgiving...

Have fun and test those grey cells...

Time for a test now to see how good a quizzer you are. Would you make it to the big money on a TV quiz?

Phones to one side – no Google or Wikipedia, no matter how much you are tempted!

Answer as many as you can on each page, then you can immediately check those answers by turning over to the next page. Keep a running total of how you are doing.

Your eventual score will be out of a possible 120.

You can keep dipping in and out until you've attempted to answer them all.

Round 1

1. What was the name of The Beatles' manager who bravely predicted in 1962 that his then unknown scruffy scouse discoveries would one day be bigger than Elvis?

2. Who connects the title of Roy Orbison's song 'Pretty Woman' with the 1991 film *Hook*, Steven Spielberg's version of the Peter Pan story?

3. 'Saturday Night's Alright for Fighting' was a big 1973 hit for Sir Elton John. Somehow though he doesn't seem the sort to be an authority on Saturday-night backstreet punch-ups, but then he didn't actually write those lyrics. Who did?

4. Will Smith played a civilian alien hunter in the 1997 movie *Men in Black*, but he'd played a military alien hunter a year before in which Hollywood blockbuster?

5. Neil Diamond starred in the 1980 film *The Jazz Singer*. In it he fell out with his rabbi father who didn't want him to become a pop star. Which unlikely acting legend played his father?

1. What was the name of The Beatles' manager who bravely predicted in 1962 that his then unknown scruffy scouse discoveries would one day be bigger than Elvis?
ANSWER: **Brian Epstein**
(He had no experience of managing pop groups, being the manager of a Liverpool record shop...)

2. Who connects the title of Roy Orbison's song 'Pretty Woman' with the 1991 film *Hook*, Steven Spielberg's version of the Peter Pan story?
ANSWER: **Julia Roberts**
(She played Richard Gere's hooker with a heart in the hit film Pretty Woman, and she also played Tinkerbell in Hook.)

3. 'Saturday Night's Alright for Fighting' was a big 1973 hit for Sir Elton John. Somehow though he doesn't seem the sort to be an authority on Saturday-night backstreet punch-ups, but then he didn't actually write those lyrics. Who did?
ANSWER: **Bernie Taupin**
(Bernie must be one of the richest unknown faces in the world, having co-written most of Elton's classic hits, without ever appearing on stage or record with him.)

4. Will Smith played a civilian alien hunter in the 1997 movie *Men in Black*, but he'd played a military alien hunter a year before in which Hollywood blockbuster?
ANSWER: **Independence Day**
(So named because aliens invaded Earth on the 4th of July. Just think – if they'd invaded in February, the film would have had to be called Pancake Day...)

5. Neil Diamond starred in the 1980 film *The Jazz Singer*. In it he fell out with his rabbi father who didn't want him to become a pop star. Which unlikely acting legend played his father?
ANSWER: **Sir Laurence Olivier**
(Olivier wrote a long letter of apology to the director when he was overheard in a restaurant saying the film was a pile of crap and he'd only done it for the money...)

6. 'Mrs Robinson' by Simon & Garfunkel was the theme song from the classic Dustin Hoffman movie *The Graduate*, but who played Mrs Robinson?

7. Which famous British female singer, who rose to fame in the 60s, actually shares her surname with Barry White, but is better known by a totally contradictory name?

8. 'Who Are You' by The Who was the signature tune to *CSI: Vegas*. One member of the band actually played a part in the series. Who was that?

9. The song 'I Got You Babe' first introduced Cher to the world, as one half of the duo Sonny & Cher. Cher's full name is Cherilyn Sarkisian LaPiere. Sonny's first name was really Salvatore, but he shared his surname with the lead singer of a world-famous rock band. What is that name?

10. The weird and wonderful *Addams Family* household had a monosyllabic butler. What was he called?

6. 'Mrs Robinson' by Simon & Garfunkel was the theme song from the classic Dustin Hoffman movie *The Graduate*, but who played Mrs Robinson?
ANSWER: **Anne Bancroft**
(Wife of comedy film-maker Mel Brooks.)

7. Which famous British female singer, who rose to fame in the 60s, actually shares her surname with Barry White, but is better known by a totally contradictory name?
ANSWER: **Cilla Black**
(Priscilla Maria Veronica White came to the attention of The Beatles' new manager Brian Epstein when she was the cloakroom attendant at the now legendary Cavern Club.)

8. 'Who Are You' by The Who was the signature tune to *CSI: Vegas*. One member of the band actually played a part in the series. Who was that?
ANSWER: **Roger Daltrey**
(Daltrey guest-starred as Mickey Dunn, a ruthless Las Vegas mobster...)

9. The song 'I Got You Babe' first introduced Cher to the world, as one half of the duo Sonny & Cher. Cher's full name is Cherilyn Sarkisian LaPiere. Sonny's first name was really Salvatore, but he shared his surname with the lead singer of a world-famous rock band. What is that name?
ANSWER: **Bono**
(It's a good job they took stage names – Sonny & Cher is a lot catchier than Salvatore Bono and Cherilyn Sarkisian La Piere.)

10. The weird and wonderful *Addams Family* household had a monosyllabic butler. What was he called?
ANSWER: **Lurch**
(The family were: Morticia and Gomez Addams ... daughter Wednesday and son Pugsley ... not forgetting Uncle Fester...)

11. Name the 1965 James Brown hit that featured the immortal line: "He's doing the Monkey, the Mashed Potatoes / Jump back Jack, see you later alligator?"

12. Which *Monty Python* luminary put a 'Q' in Bond?

13. David Bowie's career really went stratospheric in 1972 when he reinvented himself as an alien androgynous alter ego with his backing band The Spiders from Mars. What name did he give that alter-ego?

14. In terms of the British monarchy what was uniquely significant about the year 1936?

15. Rod Stewart is famous for the string of stunning blondes that have been on his arm over the years – but how many times has he actually been married?

11. Name the 1965 James Brown hit that featured the immortal line: "He's doing the Monkey, the Mashed Potatoes / Jump back Jack, see you later alligator?"
ANSWER: **'Papa's Got a Brand New Bag'**
(The bizarre lyrics of the first verse are: "Come here sister ... Papa's in the swing / He ain't too hip ... about that new breed babe / He ain't no drag / Papa's got a brand new bag..." Ahhhhh! They don't write songs like they used to in the good ol' days...)

12. Which *Monty Python* luminary put a 'Q' in Bond?
ANSWER: **John Cleese**
(Cleese played the eccentric head of gadgets 'Q' in a Bond film, Die Another Day, with Pierce Brosnan as Bond. He took over from Desmond Llewelyn who had played 'Q' for 36 years.)

13. David Bowie's career really went stratospheric in 1972 when he reinvented himself as an alien androgynous alter ego with his backing band The Spiders from Mars. What name did he give that alter-ego?
ANSWER: **Ziggy Stardust**
(The album was called The Rise and Fall of Ziggy Stardust & The Spiders from Mars, and he even went on tour around the world as Ziggy Stardust.)

14. In terms of the British monarchy what was uniquely significant about the year 1936?
ANSWER: **The UK had three different kings that year**
(King George V, who died in January 1936 ... King Edward VIII replaced his father, until he abdicated in December 1936 ... to be replaced by his younger brother, King George VI. Edward VIII was one of our shortest reigning monarchs, being King for just 326 days.)

15. Rod Stewart is famous for the string of stunning blondes that have been on his arm over the years – but how many times has he actually been married?
ANSWER: **Three times**
(Alana Hamilton... Rachel Hunter... Penny Lancaster...)

16. What was the full name and rank of the character nicknamed 'The Pizza Man' in the American TV series *Hill Street Blues*?

17. Kylie Minogue famously played Charlene in *Neighbours*. Her on-screen marriage to Scott, played by Jason Donovan, was watched by 20 million viewers in Britain alone. But what was the duet called that got the lovebirds to the number 1 slot in 1988?

18. Which famous football pundit hosted the first ever episode of *Match of the Day*, back in 1964?

19. On which 1972 Carly Simon hit single did Mick Jagger provide backing vocals?

20. Which guest failed to turn up for an episode of *Have I Got News for You* in 1993, and was famously replaced by a tub of lard?

16. What was the full name and rank of the character nicknamed 'The Pizza Man' in the American TV series *Hill Street Blues*?
ANSWER: **Captain Frank Furillo**
(Daniel J. Travanti played Captain Frank Furillo, who was nicknamed The Pizza Man by his other half.)

17. Kylie Minogue famously played Charlene in *Neighbours*. Her on-screen marriage to Scott, played by Jason Donovan, was watched by 20 million viewers in Britain alone. But what was the duet called that got the lovebirds to the number 1 slot in 1988?
ANSWER: **'Especially For You'**
(Both became pop megastars in the 1980s thanks to Stock Aitken and Waterman's hit factory.)

18. Which famous football pundit hosted the first ever episode of *Match of the Day*, back in 1964?
ANSWER: **Kenneth Wolstenholme**
(David Coleman didn't come into the frame until 1970, then Jimmy Hill in 1973...)

19. On which 1972 Carly Simon hit single did Mick Jagger provide backing vocals?
ANSWER: **'You're So Vain'**
(Harry Nilsson was hanging around the studio with Mick and joined in as well. The song is rumoured to be about Warren Beatty who Carly had been dating.)

20. Which guest failed to turn up for an episode of *Have I Got News for You* in 1993, and was famously replaced by a tub of lard?
ANSWER: **Roy Hattersley MP**
(Nobody spotted the difference...)

21. Who wrote the theme tune 'I Could Be So Good for You' for the original George Cole version of *Minder*?

22. The original *Mission Impossible* TV series always started with a tape recording that was set to self-destruct in how many seconds?

23. Which world-famous talent show judge appeared as Wonderdog on *Top of the Pops* in 1982, promoting the one-hit-wonder: 'Ruff Mix' by Wonderdog?

24. What was the first name of Marley's Ghost in *A Christmas Carol*?

25. Who was the Carol immortalised in the 1959 Neil Sedaka hit 'Oh! Carol'?

21. Who wrote the theme tune 'I Could Be So Good for You' for the original George Cole version of *Minder*?
ANSWER: **Patricia Waterman & Gerard Kenny**
(Dennis Waterman sang the song, but didn't write it, as many people believe. It was credited as Waterman/Kenny – but it was his then wife Patricia Waterman who wrote 'I Could Be So Good for You' with Gerard Kenny. It got to number 3 in the charts in 1980.)

22. The original *Mission Impossible* TV series always started with a tape recording that was set to self-destruct in how many seconds?
ANSWER: **Five seconds**
("This tape will self-destruct in five seconds" was usually followed by the words "Good luck, Jim!" ... Jim being Jim Phelps, played by Peter Graves.)

23. Which world-famous talent show judge appeared as Wonderdog on *Top of the Pops* in 1982, promoting the one-hit-wonder: 'Ruff Mix' by Wonderdog?
ANSWER: **Simon Cowell**
(Before he was famous Cowell dressed up as Wonderdog, in a fluffy blue dog costume and a red cape to promote 'Ruff Mix' on Top of the Pops *and numerous kids' TV shows...)*

24. What was the first name of Marley's Ghost in *A Christmas Carol*?
ANSWER: **Jacob**
(Jacob Marley was Scrooge's deceased business partner and his ghost materialised to show Scrooge the errors of his ways...)

25. Who was the Carol immortalised in the 1959 Neil Sedaka hit 'Oh! Carol'?
ANSWER: **Fellow songwriter Carole King**
(She was Sedaka's then girlfriend, born Carol Joan Klein.)

26. Who created the church of scientology in 1952?

27. In Tim Burton's version of *Charlie & The Chocolate Factory*, who played Willy Wonka?

28. In *Dad's Army* Clive Dunn plays Corporal Jones. But what was old Jonesey's first name?

29. Which cereal crop is traditionally used to make the malt for whisky and beer?

30. Who famously said: "When I'm good I'm very good, but when I'm bad I'm better" ... and even more famously: "Is that a pistol in your pocket or are you just glad to see me?"?

26. Who created the church of scientology in 1952?
    ANSWER: **L. Ron Hubbard**
    (Previously a writer of pulp fiction and outlandish sci-fi stories...)

27. In Tim Burton's version of *Charlie & The Chocolate Factory*, who played Willy Wonka?
    ANSWER: **Johnny Depp**
    (Gene Wilder had previously played Willy Wonka in the 1971 film version of the classic Roald Dahl story.)

28. In *Dad's Army* Clive Dunn plays Corporal Jones. But what was old Jonesey's first name?
    ANSWER: **Jack**
    (Jack Jones the butcher.)

29. Which cereal crop is traditionally used to make the malt for whisky and beer?
    ANSWER: **Barley**

30. Who famously said: "When I'm good I'm very good, but when I'm bad I'm better" ... and even more famously: "Is that a pistol in your pocket or are you just glad to see me?"?
    ANSWER: **Mae West**
    (She also said: "It's not the men in my life that count, it's the life in my men" ... and ... "Marriage is a fine institution – but I'm not ready for an institution" ... And they say strong women have only just been liberated!)

31. Who connects Michael Jackson's classic hit 'Thriller' with the horror films *The House of Wax* and *The Fly*?

32. Which spacecraft landed on Mars in August 2012?

33. Overnight pop sensation *Jedward* were identical twins. What is their shared surname?

34. YMCA is an acronym for the Young Men's Christian Association, but what does the acronym YOLO stand for in text and internet slang?

35. Percy Weasley was Ron Weasley's brother in the Harry Potter films, but who played Mr & Mrs Weasley?

31. Who connects Michael Jackson's classic hit 'Thriller' with the horror films *The House of Wax* and *The Fly*?
ANSWER: **Vincent Price**
(Price did the spooky voice-over on 'Thriller' and starred in The House of Wax *and the original 1958 version of* The Fly.)

32. Which spacecraft landed on Mars in August 2012?
ANSWER: **Curiosity**
(Two-year mission to search for traces of life.)

33. Overnight pop sensation *Jedward* were identical twins. What is their shared surname?
ANSWER: **Grimes**
(Their first names are John and Edward, which combined make Jedward. Do you think if they'd been called Tom and Roger they would have gone out on the road as 'Todger'?)

34. YMCA is an acronym for the Young Men's Christian Association, but what does the acronym YOLO stand for in text and internet slang?
ANSWER: **You Only Live Once**
(The expression has been described as 'Carpe Diem' for stupid people...)

35. Percy Weasley was Ron Weasley's brother in the Harry Potter films, but who played Mr & Mrs Weasley?
ANSWER: **Mark Williams / Julie Walters**
(Mark Williams was famous for his camp catchphrase 'Suit you sir!' in The Fast Show.)

36. Tina Turner was born over 80 years ago in which town in Tennessee? ... I'll give you a clue: its 'City Limits' gave her a Top 5 hit in 1973.

37. The 'Uptown Girl' Billy Joel sang about in his 1983 number 1 hit was in fact his real-life supermodel girlfriend. Who was she?

38. With which famous pop act did 1960s singing star Dusty Springfield find chart fame again in the late 1980s?

39. Which classic album connects Elton John with *The Wizard of Oz*?

40. In which classic BBC television series did Kylie Minogue make a guest appearance as a waitress on The Titanic, called Astrid Peth?

36. Tina Turner was born over 80 years ago in which town in Tennessee? ... I'll give you a clue: its 'City Limits' gave her a Top 5 hit in 1973.
ANSWER: **'Nutbush'**
('Nutbush City Limits' was the last single credited as Ike & Tina Turner, before she divorced her abusive other half.)

37. The 'Uptown Girl' Billy Joel sang about in his 1983 number 1 hit was in fact his real-life supermodel girlfriend. Who was she?
ANSWER: **Christie Brinkley**
(His wife-to-be.)

38. With which famous pop act did 1960s singing star Dusty Springfield find chart fame again in the late 1980s?
ANSWER: **The Pet Shop Boys**
('What Have I Done to Deserve This', 'Nothing Has Been Proved', and 'In Private' were all hit collaborations.)

39. Which classic album connects Elton John with *The Wizard of Oz*?
ANSWER: **Goodbye Yellow Brick Road**
(The album cover features Elton precariously heading off down the famed uneven cobbled road in towering platform boots. Brave or what?!)

40. In which classic BBC television series did Kylie Minogue make a guest appearance as a waitress on The Titanic, called Astrid Peth?
ANSWER: **Dr Who**
(2007 Christmas Special. Kylie just guest-starred in that one episode as David Tennant's short-lived companion. The Titanic was a spaceship.)

41. Robbie Williams remade the Frank & Nancy Sinatra hit 'Somethin' Stupid' in 2001 with a famous Hollywood actress? Who was she?

42. Keith Richards seems like a walking miracle, to have survived all the excesses of his wild life in The Rolling Stones, but what sort of a tree was nearly the death of him in 2006?

43. The Gibb brothers were better known as The Bee Gees, but by what name are the brothers Barry David Elliott and Paul Harman Elliott better known?

44. Which chocolate bar used to claim that it was "the sweet you can eat between meals without ruining your appetite"?

45. In Alan Bennett's autobiographical film of 2015, who played *The Lady in the Van*?

41. Robbie Williams remade the Frank & Nancy Sinatra hit 'Somethin' Stupid' in 2001 with a famous Hollywood actress? Who was she?
ANSWER: **Nicole Kidman**
(It was the Christmas number 1 that year.)

42. Keith Richards seems like a walking miracle, to have survived all the excesses of his wild life in The Rolling Stones, but what sort of a tree was nearly the death of him in 2006?
ANSWER: **Coconut tree**
(He was holidaying in Fiji, fell out of the coconut tree he was climbing, and cracked his head on the trunk as he landed.)

43. The Gibb brothers were better known as The Bee Gees, but by what name are the brothers Barry David Elliott and Paul Harman Elliott better known?
ANSWER: **The Chuckle Brothers**
(If you got that right it's a point "to you … to me"…)

44. Which chocolate bar used to claim that it was "the sweet you can eat between meals without ruining your appetite"?
ANSWER: **Milky Way**
(Strange marketing ploy – a snack that makes you put on weight, but leaves you just as hungry as you were to start with!)

45. In Alan Bennett's autobiographical film of 2015, who played *The Lady in the Van*?
ANSWER: **Dame Maggie Smith**
(The true story of eccentric Mary Shepherd who parked her van in Alan Bennett's drive in London, and lived there for 15 years.)

46. In 1972 Hollywood released a scary thriller called *Ben*, which featured Michael Jackson singing the title song over the end credits, but what was Ben?

47. What were the real surnames of legendary comedy double act Morecambe & Wise?

48. The band UB40 named themselves after a government form. What did 'UB' stand for on that form?

49. Which BBC television programme was responsible for making spicy Reggae Reggae Sauce a big hit in 2007?

50. 'Rule the World' by Take That was the fifth best-selling single of 2007. How many of them were there in the line-up of Take That at that time?

46. In 1972 Hollywood released a scary thriller called *Ben*, which featured Michael Jackson singing the title song over the end credits, but what was Ben?
ANSWER: ***A rat***
(It was that old tried and tested Hollywood formula – boy meets rat, boy finds out rat is the leader of a swarm of killer rodents, boy still loves rat...)

47. What were the real surnames of legendary comedy double act Morecambe & Wise?
ANSWER: **John Eric BARTHOLOMEW and Ernest WISEMAN**

48. The band UB40 named themselves after a government form. What did 'UB' stand for on that form?
ANSWER: **Unemployment Benefit**
(A UB40 had to be filled in by anybody signing on for the dole, and the band were all unemployed when they formed in 1978.)

49. Which BBC television programme was responsible for making spicy Reggae Reggae Sauce a big hit in 2007?
ANSWER: **Dragon's Den**
(Rastafarian musician Levi Roots persuaded two Dragons to invest in his now massively successful hot sauce.)

50. 'Rule the World' by Take That was the fifth best-selling single of 2007. How many of them were there in the line-up of Take That at that time?
ANSWER: **Four**
(Gary Barlow, Howard Donald, Jason Orange, Mark Owen.)

51. With which American artist did Ed Sheeran collaborate on a hit single called 'Everything Has Changed' in 2013?

52. *Tom Jones* is a scandalous tale of promiscuity, debauchery and lust. Obviously we're talking about the novel, first published in 1749. But who wrote it?

53. Mick Jagger has eight children by five different mothers, as well as his countless other high-profile relationships, but how many times has he actually been legally married?

54. Which member of the cast of American sitcom *Friends* took over from Jeremy Clarkson on a long-running BBC series?

55. Who was the first chairman of comedy panel game *Would I Lie to You*, from 2007 to 2008?

51. With which American artist did Ed Sheeran collaborate on a hit single called 'Everything Has Changed' in 2013?
ANSWER: **Taylor Swift**
(They performed the song live together on Britain's Got Talent, *but, surprisingly, they didn't win.)*

52. *Tom Jones* is a scandalous tale of promiscuity, debauchery and lust. Obviously we're talking about the novel, first published in 1749. But who wrote it?
ANSWER: **Henry Fielding**
(The full title of the novel is: The History of Tom Jones, a Foundling.*)*

53. Mick Jagger has eight children by five different mothers, as well as his countless other high-profile relationships, but how many times has he actually been legally married?
ANSWER: **Only once (to Bianca Jagger)**
(An unofficial wedding to Jerry Hall was declared invalid, unlawful and null & void by The High Court in 1999.)

54. Which member of the cast of American sitcom *Friends* took over from Jeremy Clarkson on a long-running BBC series?
ANSWER: **Matt LeBlanc**
*(*Top Gear.*)*

55. Who was the first chairman of comedy panel game *Would I Lie to You*, from 2007 to 2008?
ANSWER: **Angus Deayton**
(Rob Brydon has done it ever since.

56. What type of food is 'paneer' on an Indian menu?

57. Which Hollywood heart-throb made a guest appearance on *Friends,* as Will Colbert and was married, at the time, to one of the regular team?

58. Neil Diamond first came to prominence as a songwriter, not a singer. Which song did he write that launched the pop careers of The Monkees in 1967?

59. One of David Bowie's first ever singles was a silly novelty song which bombed in 1967. But, to his embarrassment, it became a Top 10 hit when re-released by the record company in 1973, after Bowie had attained super-stardom. What was that single?

60. What is the correct name for the *Monty Python's Flying Circus* theme tune, composed in 1893?

56. What type of food is 'paneer' on an Indian menu?
   ANSWER: **Cheese**
   (As in 'sag paneer' – spinach with cheese)

57. Which Hollywood heart-throb made a guest appearance on
   Friends, as Will Colbert and was married, at the time, to one of
   the regular team?
   ANSWER: **Brad Pitt**
   (then married to Jennifer Aniston)

58. Neil Diamond first came to prominence as a songwriter, not a
   singer. Which song did he write that launched the pop careers of
   The Monkees in 1967?
   ANSWER: **'I'm a Believer'**
   *(He wrote other songs for The Monkees, but 'I'm a Believer' gave
   them their first number 1 hit.)*

59. One of David Bowie's first ever singles was a silly novelty song
   which bombed in 1967. But, to his embarrassment, it became a
   Top 10 hit when re-released by the record company in 1973, after
   Bowie had attained super-stardom. What was that single?
   ANSWER: **'The Laughing Gnome'**
   (It featured such memorable lyrics as:
   "Haven't you got a gnome to go to?"
   *"Didn't they teach you to get your hair cut at school? You look like
   a rolling gnome."*
   "No, not at the London School of Eco-gnomics"
   ... Nice one David! Credibility totally unscathed...)

60. What is the correct name for the *Monty Python's Flying Circus*
   theme tune, composed in 1893?
   ANSWER: **'The Liberty Bell'**
   (It's an American military march composed by John Philip Sousa.)

61. Name the Quentin Tarantino film which revitalised John Travolta's waning movie career in 1994?

62. Dick Turpin was a notorious highwayman who was executed in York in 1739. What was the name of his horse on which he supposedly rode from London to York in less than 24 hours?

63. What was the currency used in Greece before they adopted the Euro in 2002?

64. What does the acronym GPS stand for when it's referring to sat-nav equipment?

(NB: I wrote this last question for a BBC TV show, to test the expert knowledge of the man who was then in charge of the Liverpool Beatles Museum. He got it wrong, so give yourself a gold star if you get this one right!)

65. Which is the only officially-released Beatles' 1960s studio album to feature nothing but Lennon/ McCartney compositions?

61. Name the Quentin Tarantino film which revitalised John Travolta's waning movie career in 1994?
ANSWER: **Pulp Fiction**
(John Travolta was nominated for the Best Actor Oscar for Pulp Fiction. *But the Oscar that year actually went to Tom Hanks for his portrayal of Forrest Gump.)*

62. Dick Turpin was a notorious highwayman who was executed in York in 1739. What was the name of his horse on which he supposedly rode from London to York in less than 24 hours?
ANSWER: **Black Bess**
(Turpin stole Black Bess at gunpoint from a man called Major, swapping her for the clapped-out old nag he used to ride.)

63. What was the currency used in Greece before they adopted the Euro in 2002?
ANSWER: **Drachma**
(The word Drachma came from a Greek verb meaning "to grasp" – referring to a handful of 6 silver sticks which were grasped as currency as far back as 1100 BC.)

64. What does the acronym GPS stand for when it's referring to sat-nav equipment?
ANSWER: **Global Positioning System**

65. Which is the only officially-released Beatles' 1960s studio album to feature nothing but Lennon/McCartney compositions?
ANSWER: **A Hard Day's Night**
(All their other albums feature covers or George Harrison compositions, and the occasional one by Ringo.)

Round 2 – multiple-choice

1. In the TV series *Blackadder Goes Forth*, which character was played by Tim McInnerny?

    A. Captain Sweetheart   B. Captain Flashheart
    C. Captain Honey   D. Captain Darling

2. What was the name of the character played by Sigourney Weaver in the *Alien* movie franchise?

    A. Dallas   B. Ripley
    C. Lambert   D. Parker

3. Who starred opposite Patrick Swayze in the hit 1987 film *Dirty Dancing*?

    A. Jennifer Grey   B. Jennifer Beale
    C. Jennifer Tilly   D. Jennifer Aniston

4. Onions make you cry when you cut into them because the vapour produces which of the following in your eye?

    A. Acetic acid   B. Lactic acid
    C. Citric acid   D. Sulphuric acid

5. Which European country produces Mateus Rose wine?

    A. France   B. Italy
    C. Spain   D. Portugal

1. In the TV series *Blackadder Goes Forth*, which character was played by Tim McInnerny?

   A. Captain Sweetheart   B. Captain Flashheart
   C. Captain Honey   D. Captain Darling

   ANSWER: *D - Captain Darling*

2. What was the name of the character played by Sigourney Weaver in the *Alien* movie franchise?

   A. Dallas   B. Ripley
   C. Lambert   D. Parker

   ANSWER: *B - Ripley*

3. Who starred opposite Patrick Swayze in the hit 1987 film *Dirty Dancing*?

   A. Jennifer Grey   B. Jennifer Beale
   C. Jennifer Tilly   D. Jennifer Aniston

   ANSWER: *A - Jennifer Grey*

4. Onions make you cry when you cut into them because the vapour produces which of the following in your eye?

   A. Acetic acid   B. Lactic acid
   C. Citric acid   D. Sulphuric acid

   ANSWER: *D - Sulphuric acid!!*

5. Which European country produces Mateus Rose wine?

   A. France   B. Italy
   C. Spain   D. Portugal

   ANSWER: *D - Portugal*

6. What makes the cocktail 'A Pink Lady' pink?

   A. Angostura bitters   B. Cranberry juice
   C. Grenadine   D. Maraschino cherry
                                          extract

7. Which city hosted the summer Olympic Games in 1904?

   A. Paris   B. Athens
   C. Rome   D. London

8. Which Shakespearian play begins with the words "If music be the food of love play on…"?

   A. Twelfth Night   B. A Midsummer Night's
                                         Dream
   C. The Taming of   D. Romeo & Juliet
      the Shrew

9. Which TV doctor was played by Sylvester McCoy?

   A. Dr Kildare   B. Dr Finlay
   C. Dr Who   D. Dr 'Bones' McCoy

10. Which of these national leaders was the only one alive in 100 BC?

   A. Alexander the Great   B. Julius Caesar
   C. Attila the Hun   D. Cleopatra

6. What makes the cocktail 'A Pink Lady' pink?

   A. Angostura bitters   B. Cranberry juice
   C. Grenadine   D. Maraschino cherry extract

   *ANSWER: **C - Grenadine***

7. Which city hosted the summer Olympic Games in 1904?

   A. Paris   B. Athens
   C. Rome   D. London

   *ANSWER: **D - London***
   (then again in 1948 and of course 2012.)

8. Which Shakespearian play begins with the words "If music be the food of love play on…"?

   A. Twelfth Night   B. A Midsummer Night's Dream
   C. The Taming of the Shrew   D. Romeo & Juliet

   *ANSWER: **A - Twelfth Night***
   (Spoken by Duke Orsino.)

9. Which TV doctor was played by Sylvester McCoy?

   A. Dr Kildare   B. Dr Finlay
   C. Dr Who   D. Dr 'Bones' McCoy

   *ANSWER: **C - Dr Who***
   (from 1987 to 1989)

10. Which of these national leaders was the only one alive in 100 BC?

    A. Alexander the Great   B. Julius Caesar
    C. Attila the Hun   D. Cleopatra

    *ANSWER: **B - Julius Caesar, who was born in 100 BC***

11. The Harry Nilsson song 'Everybody's Talking' became a hit in 1969 after it featured in which iconic Hollywood movie?

    A. Midnight Cowboy   B. MASH
    C. Love Story   D. Butch Cassidy
                               and the Sundance Kid

12. Which of the gospel writers is the patron saint of Venice?

    A. Matthew   B. Mark
    C. Luke   D. John

13. Where did Manchester United play their home matches between 1941 and 1949?

    A. Elland Road   B. Anfield
    C. Salford Rugby Club   D. Maine Road

14. What was the 'Al' short for in the commonly used name of Chicago gangster Al Capone?

    A. Aloysius   B. Alfredo
    C. Alphonse   D. Alberto

15. Which of the following belongs to the same family of plants as the lethally poisonous 'deadly nightshade'?

    A. Tomato   B. Crab apple
    C. Rhubarb   D. Horseradish

11. The Harry Nilsson song 'Everybody's Talking' became a hit in 1969 after it featured in which iconic Hollywood movie?

   A.   Midnight Cowboy
   B.   MASH
   C.   Love Story
   D.   Butch Cassidy and the Sundance Kid

   *ANSWER: **A - Midnight Cowboy***

12. Which of the gospel writers is the patron saint of Venice?

   A.   Matthew
   B.   Mark
   C.   Luke
   D.   John

   *ANSWER: **B - Saint Mark***

13. Where did Manchester United play their home matches between 1941 and 1949?

   A.   Elland Road
   B.   Anfield
   C.   Salford Rugby Club
   D.   Maine Road

   *ANSWER: **D - Maine Road***
   (Old Trafford had been bombed in WW2 and they shared Maine Road with their arch-rivals Manchester City while Old Trafford was being re-built.)

14. What was the 'Al' short for in the commonly used name of Chicago gangster Al Capone?

   A.   Aloysius
   B.   Alfredo
   C.   Alphonse
   D.   Alberto

   *ANSWER: **C - Alphonse Gabriel Capone***

15. Which of the following belongs to the same family of plants as the lethally poisonous 'deadly nightshade'?

   A.   Tomato
   B.   Crab apple
   C.   Rhubarb
   D.   Horseradish

   *ANSWER: **A - Tomato***
   (As does aubergine, potato, chilli pepper and tobacco.)

16. On which river does the city of Vienna stand?

    A. Danube   B. Rhone
    C. Rhine   D. Weser

17. Which fictional sailor was the Captain of a ship
    called The Black Pig?

    A. Captain Hook   B. Popeye
    C. Captain Pugwash   D. Long John Silver

18. In Australia The Melbourne Cup is their most
    prestigious event in which sport?

    A. Rugby   B. Horse racing
    C. Australian rules football D. Cricket

19. Which city was the first to have an underground
    railway system?

    A. Paris   B. London
    C. Glasgow   D. New York

20. Which of these is not a nickname for the Devil?

    A. Old Nick   B. Old Harry
    C. Old George   D. Old Ned

16. On which river does the city of Vienna stand?

A. Danube   B. Rhone
C. Rhine   D. Weser

*ANSWER: **A - Danube***

17. Which fictional sailor was the Captain of a ship called The Black Pig?

A. Captain Hook   B. Popeye
C. Captain Pugwash   D. Long John Silver

*ANSWER: **C - Captain Pugwash***
(From the BBC cartoon series of the same name)

18. In Australia The Melbourne Cup is their most prestigious event in which sport?

A. Rugby   B. Horse racing
C. Australian rules football   D. Cricket

*ANSWER: **B - Horse racing***

19. Which city was the first to have an underground railway system?

A. Paris   B. London
C. Glasgow   D. New York

*ANSWER: **B - London***

20. Which of these is not a nickname for the Devil?

A. Old Nick   B. Old Harry
C. Old George   D. Old Ned

*ANSWER: **C - Old George***

21. Which football team did television's Alf Garnett famously support?

A. Arsenal
B. Tottenham Hotspur
C. Queens Park Rangers
D. West Ham United

22. Which one of these is a quadruped?

A. A rectangle
B. A cow
C. A four-wheeled bike
D. A manoeuvre in ballet or skating

23. Who is the youngest of these four famous women?

A. Vanessa Feltz
B. Annie Lennox
C. Theresa May
D. Dawn French

24. Who wrote the children's story *The Old Man of Lochnagar*?

A. Prince Edward
B. Fergie, The Duchess of York
C. Camilla, Queen Consort
D. King Charles III

25. Which Olympic gold medallist became the MP for Falmouth and Camborne in 1992?

A. Daley Thompson
B. Sebastian Coe
C. Steve Ovett
D. Dame Kelly Holmes

21. Which football team did television's Alf Garnett famously support?

    A. Arsenal   B. Tottenham Hotspur
    C. Queens Park Rangers   D. West Ham United

    *ANSWER: **D - West Ham***

22. Which one of these is a quadruped?

    A. A rectangle   B. A cow
    C. A four-wheeled bike   D. A manoeuvre in ballet or
    skating

    *ANSWER: **B - Cow***
    (Because it has four legs.)

23. Who is the youngest of these four famous women?

    A. Vanessa Feltz   B. Annie Lennox
    C. Theresa May   D. Dawn French

    *ANSWER: **A - Vanessa Feltz***
    (Dawn French next youngest, then Theresa May, then Annie Lennox.)

24. Who wrote the children's story *The Old Man of Lochnagar*?

    A. Prince Edward   B. Fergie,
                                     The Duchess of York
    C. Camilla,   D. King Charles III
        Queen Consort

    *ANSWER: **D - King Charles III***

25. Which Olympic gold medallist became the MP for Falmouth and Camborne in 1992?

    A. Daley Thompson   B. Sebastian Coe
    C. Steve Ovett   D. Dame Kelly Holmes

    *ANSWER: **B - Sebastian Coe, now Lord Coe***

26. What was the nationality of the composer Gustav Holst?

   A. English
   C. Russian
   B. German
   D. Norwegian

27. Which of these is not a highly venomous snake?

   A. Death's Head
   C. Cottonmouth
   B. Copperhead
   D. Boomslang

28. What did the Ancient Romans call an open-air marketplace or central public square?

   A. Pantheon
   C. Forum
   B. Basilica
   D. Hippodrome

29. Which of these is not a town or city in Texas, USA?
   A. Paris
   C. Athens
   B. Brussels
   D. Dublin

30. In the 1983 Stephen King horror film *Christine*, who or what was Christine?

   A. A killer car
   C. A killer child
   B. A killer spider
   D. A killer doll

26. What was the nationality of the composer Gustav Holst?

A. English
B. German
C. Russian
D. Norwegian

ANSWER: *A - English*
(He was born in Cheltenham, Gloucestershire.)

27. Which of these is not a highly venomous snake?

A. Death's Head
B. Copperhead
C. Cottonmouth
D. Boomslang

ANSWER: *A - Death's Head*
(Which is a poor harmless moth!)

28. What did the Ancient Romans call an open-air marketplace or central public square?

A. Pantheon
B. Basilica
C. Forum
D. Hippodrome

ANSWER: *C - Forum*

29. Which of these is not a town or city in Texas, USA?

A. Paris
B. Brussels
C. Athens
D. Dublin

ANSWER: *B - Brussels*
(All the others really are!)

30. In the 1983 Stephen King horror film *Christine*, who or what was Christine?

A. A killer car
B. A killer spider
C. A killer child
D. A killer doll

ANSWER: *A - A killer car*

31. What name is given to the Japanese martial art of swordsmanship practised using bamboo staves?

A. Jiu Jitsu
B. Aikido
C. Taekwondo
D. Kendo

32. Which of these Wilsons has never been in The Beach Boys?

A. Brian Wilson
B. Owen Wilson
C. Dennis Wilson
D. Carl Wilson

33. In which city could you visit the legendary Topkapi Palace?

A. Istanbul
B. Rome
C. Toronto
D. Sydney

34. Which of these is not one of King Charles's three middle names?

A. George
B. Arthur
C. William
D. Philip

35. Who played Thelma in the classic Ridley Scott road movie *Thelma & Louise*?

A. Geena Davis
B. Annette Benning
C. Susan Sarandon
D. Sally Field

31. What name is given to the Japanese martial art of swordsmanship practised using bamboo staves?

A. Jiu Jitsu
B. Aikido
C. Taekwondo
D. Kendo

ANSWER: **D - Kendo**

32. Which of these Wilsons has never been in The Beach Boys?

A. Brian Wilson
B. Owen Wilson
C. Dennis Wilson
D. Carl Wilson

ANSWER: **B - Owen Wilson**
(He's a Hollywood comedy actor.)

33. In which city could you visit the legendary Topkapi Palace?

A. Istanbul
B. Rome
C. Toronto
D. Sydney

ANSWER: **A - Istanbul**

34. Which of these is not one of King Charles's three middle names?
A. George
B. Arthur
C. William
D. Philip

ANSWER: **C - William**
(He is: Charles Philip Arthur George Windsor.)

35. Who played Thelma in the classic Ridley Scott road movie *Thelma & Louise*?

A. Geena Davis
B. Annette Benning
C. Susan Sarandon
D. Sally Field

ANSWER: **A - Geena Davis**
(Louise was Susan Sarandon.)

36. Which children's TV characters ate blue string pudding?

    A. The Flumps   B. The Clangers
    C. The Wombles   D. The Smurfs

37. Who is the only one of these *Strictly Come Dancing* finalists who actually won the glitter ball trophy that year?

    A. Alesha Dixon   B. Debbie McGee
    C. Louise Redknapp   D. Alexandra Burke

38. What sort of mythical character is Gandalf in JRR Tolkien's novel *Lord of the Rings*?

    A. Elf   B. Dragon
    C. Wizard   D. Hobbit

39. Which of these is the only one which is not an African country?

    A. The Seychelles   B. Morocco
    C. Yemen   D. Egypt

40. Which of these is not a character in Lewis Carroll's classic children's book *Alice's Adventures in Wonderland*?

    A. The March Hare   B. The Cheshire Cat
    C. Tweedledee   D. The King of Hearts

36. Which children's TV characters ate blue string pudding?

 A. The Flumps
 B. The Clangers
 C. The Wombles
 D. The Smurfs

*ANSWER: **B - The Clangers***

37. Who is the only one of these *Strictly Come Dancing* finalists who actually won the glitter ball trophy that year?

 A. Alesha Dixon
 B. Debbie McGee
 C. Louise Redknapp
 D. Alexandra Burke

*ANSWER: **A - Alesha Dixon***

38. What sort of mythical character is Gandalf in JRR Tolkien's novel *Lord of the Rings*?

 A. Elf
 B. Dragon
 C. Wizard
 D. Hobbit

*ANSWER: **C - Wizard***

39. Which of these is the only one which is not an African country?

 A. The Seychelles
 B. Morocco
 C. Yemen
 D. Egypt

ANSWER: C - Yemen
(It's an Arab republic in the Middle East.)

40. Which of these is not a character in Lewis Carroll's classic children's book *Alice's Adventures in Wonderland*?

 A. The March Hare
 B. The Cheshire Cat
 C. Tweedledee
 D. The King of Hearts

ANSWER: C - Tweedledee
(Tweedledum and Tweedledee only appear in the sequel Through the Looking Glass.)

41. Who is the youngest?

    A. Paul McCartney   B. Michael Palin
    C. Mick Jagger   D. Former PM John Major

42. Which of these was not a famous American TV
    detective?

    A. Quincy   B. Ironside
    C. Kojak   D. Columbo

43. Which of these classic multi-movie franchises has
    Michael Caine never starred in?

    A. Jaws   B. Austin Powers
    C. Jurassic Park   D. The Muppets

44. Where was The Magna Carta signed?

    A. Near Windsor Castle   B. Near Hampton Court
    C. Near the Tower   D. Near Buckingham
       of London   Palace

45. Kopi Luwak are beans which have been swallowed
    and then excreted by a small mammal in their dung.
    What do humans then use them for?

    A. Making Amazonian tribal necklaces
    B. Cultivating tapeworms for medical research
    C. Making a cup of coffee
    D. Distilling an illegal hallucinatory drug

41. Who is the youngest?

A. Paul McCartney B. Michael Palin
C. Mick Jagger D. Former PM John Major

ANSWER: *C - Mick Jagger*
(Michael Palin and John Major are only older than Mick by a few months. Macca is the oldest.)

42. Which of these was not a famous American TV detective?

A. Quincy B. Ironside
C. Kojak D. Columbo

ANSWER: A - Quincy
(Quincy was a medical examiner who helped the police solve crimes.)

43. Which of these classic multi-movie franchises has Michael Caine never starred in?

A. Jaws B. Austin Powers
C. Jurassic Park D. The Muppets

ANSWER: *C - Jurassic Park*
(Michael Caine was in Jaws 4 ... Austin Powers: Goldmember ... and The Muppet Christmas Carol.)

44. Where was The Magna Carta signed?

A. Near Windsor Castle B. Near Hampton Court
C. Near the Tower D. Near Buckingham Palace
   of London

ANSWER: *A - Near Windsor Castle (Runnymede)*

45. Kopi Luwak are beans which have been swallowed and then excreted by a small mammal in their dung. What do humans then use them for?

A. Making Amazonian tribal necklaces
B. Cultivating tapeworms for medical research
C. Making a cup of coffee
D. Distilling an illegal hallucinatory drug

ANSWER: *C - Making a cup of coffee*
(It's the most expensive coffee in the world! Mmmm! Lovely! Hang on – it tastes c**p!)

46. Tom Cruise is the actor's stage name. His real name is which one of the following?

    A. Timothy Crusoe III   B. Thomas Mapother IV
    C. Thomas Creosote II   D. Thomas Mulholland V

47. Which of these is not a cartoon dog?

    A. Pluto   B. Boo-Boo
    C. Scrappy-Doo   D. Snoopy

48. Approximately how long did Britney Spears' first marriage last?

    A. Just over a week   B. 27 hours
    C. 55 hours   D. 4½ days

49. Which of these wasn't one of Bob Geldof's offspring?

    A. Fifi Trixibelle   B. Candy Apple
    C. Peaches Honeyblossom D. Little Pixie

50. Which *Eastenders* character shot Phil Mitchell in 2001?

    A. Pauline   B. Dot
    C. Lisa   D. Laura

46. Tom Cruise is the actor's stage name. His real name is which one of the following?

A. Timothy Crusoe III
B. Thomas Mapother IV
C. Thomas Creosote II
D. Thomas Mulholland V

ANSWER: *B - Thomas Mapother IV*

47. Which of these is not a cartoon dog?

A. Pluto
B. Boo-Boo
C. Scrappy-Doo
D. Snoopy

ANSWER: *B - Boo-Boo*
(Boo-Boo is a bear – Yogi Bear's side-kick)

48. Approximately how long did Britney Spears' first marriage last?

A. Just over a week
B. 27 hours
C. 55 hours
D. 4½ days

ANSWER: *C - 55 hours*

49. Which of these wasn't one of Bob Geldof's offspring?

A. Fifi Trixibelle
B. Candy Apple
C. Peaches Honeyblossom
D. Little Pixie

ANSWER: *B - Candy Apple*
(Gwyneth Paltrow & Chris Martin have a daughter called Apple.)

50. Which *Eastenders* character shot Phil Mitchell in 2001?

A. Pauline
B. Dot
C. Lisa
D. Laura

ANSWER: *C - Lisa*

51. Which of these indigenous African animals is the only one which is not one of the so-called 'Big Five'?

A. Rhinoceros
B. Buffalo
C. Leopard
D. Hippopotamus

52. Who appeared in *Coronation Street* as Mel Hutchwright?

A. Peter Kay
B. Sir Ian McKellen
C. Nigel Havers
D. Bradley Walsh

53. Who is the oldest of the late Queen Elizabeth II's grandchildren?

A. Princess Beatrice
B. Prince William
C. Zara Phillips
D. Peter Phillips

54. Former *Coronation Street* actor Davy Jones became the lead singer of The Monkees, but which British actor played Davy Jones in *The Pirates of the Caribbean* films?

A. Mackenzie Crook
B. Geoffrey Rush
C. Bill Nighy
D. Richard E. Grant

55. Renowned physicist and astronomer Professor Brian Cox was once the keyboard player for which 1990s pop band?

A. Inspiral Carpets
B. D:Ream
C. The Chemical Brothers
D. $targazers Inc

51. Which of these indigenous African animals is the only one which is not one of the so-called 'Big Five'?

A. Rhinoceros   B. Buffalo
C. Leopard   D. Hippopotamus

*ANSWER: **D - Hippopotamus***

52. Who appeared in *Coronation Street* as Mel Hutchwright?

A. Peter Kay   B. Sir Ian McKellen
C. Nigel Havers D. Bradley Walsh

*ANSWER: **B - Sir Ian McKellen***
(They have all appeared in Corrie. Peter Kay appeared as Eric Gartside ... Nigel Havers appeared as Lewis Archer ... and Bradley Walsh appeared as Danny Baldwin.)

53. Who is the oldest of the late Queen Elizabeth II's grandchildren?

A. Princess Beatrice   B. Prince William
C. Zara Phillips   D. Peter Phillips

*ANSWER: **D - Peter Phillips***

54. Former *Coronation Street* actor Davy Jones became the lead singer of The Monkees, but which British actor played Davy Jones in *The Pirates of the Caribbean* films?

A. Mackenzie Crook   B. Geoffrey Rush
C. Bill Nighy   D. Richard E. Grant

*ANSWER: **C - Bill Nighy***
(He appeared with an octopus-like thing on his face and a huge crab's claw for a left hand, so you could be forgiven for not recognising him!)

55. Renowned physicist and astronomer Professor Brian Cox was once the keyboard player for which 1990s pop band?

A. Inspiral Carpets   B. D:Ream
C. The Chemical Brothers D. $targazers Inc

*ANSWER: **B - D:Ream***

So, how did you do? If you tried to answer all the questions, in both rounds, the possible total score was 120 points.

Everybody's different and we only know what we know, but I reckon if you scored over 100 (without cheating) then you're a pretty good quizzer.

Time to apply to be on a TV quiz show and turn that hard-earned knowledge into hard-earned cash. Lots of luck!